Lead the
IDEAL Project

ENABLE JOY • ENGAGE EXCELLENCE

Paul F. Armstrong

First Edition

Edited by: Innovative Editing, LLC Lancaster, PA
Book Layout ©2017 BookDesignTemplates.com

Paul F. Armstrong/eNthusaProve, LLC
Lancaster, Pennsylvania, 17603
www.enthusaprove.com

Lead the IDEAL Project /Paul F. Armstrong. –1st ed.
ISBN: 978-1-7341962-0-7

Contents

`

Dedicated to Diana, Thomas, Joanna, Andrew

Walk joyfully through life.
And, if at times you cannot,
At least walk with faith and courage.

— Francis DeSales, 1567-1622

The IDEAL Approach
Joy + Excellence

What Is an IDEAL Project?

An IDEAL project is when:

- A human team endeavor transforms an idea into a reality.
- The endeavor is built on and builds up joy for those whose time and talents are poured into it.
- The endeavor achieves excellent results that delight those who pay for and use what the project delivers.

Why All Caps for "IDEAL"?

As you'd expect in a book called *Lead the IDEAL Project*, you're about to see the word IDEAL. A lot. Sometimes, it will be lowercased when it's merely a noun or adjective. But when it's capitalized, it's to remind you that it stands for three ideas at the same time:

First: We don't just want a project that is good; we want it to be the consummate project in both experience and delivery. In other words, we want it to be ideal in a standout way.

Second: As an acronym, it's meant to help us remember 15 key elements to achieve and accomplish the consummate project in question.

Third: It's shorthand for what our project endeavor is really about: transforming an idea to make it real. Idea to Real = IDEAL.

Do You Strive to Lead an IDEAL Project?

Are you about to be in charge of a project? Are you getting ready to be responsible –accountable – for pulling together a group of people to make something happen? Does your title sound something like Project Manager, Product Team Leader, or Program Director? Given that…

- Do you believe that your calling in leading a project team involves more than just managing costs, schedules, scopes and quality?

- Do you believe that this project is about more than just satisfying the customer(s)? Does it go further than that to delight the customer(s), achieving their vision?

- Do you want your team members to be better for being on this project rather than having served as mere resources to get a job done?

If you answered yes to these questions, then this book is your guide to put what you believe into action. You are a leader who believes that leading a team to deliver excellence is **not about managing.** To you, *it's personal*! So the IDEAL approach is designed to **help you be that personal leader you strive to be in an epic way,** by enabling joy and engaging excellence for your project.

In short, this book is intended to serve those who lead projects. Project team leaders frequently need to lead people who they don't have supervisory authority over. Knowing that – and the problems it comes with – it might be tempting to rely on carrot-and-stick motivational methods. And, sure enough, those seductive addictions may work in the short term. Yet they rarely give you long-term success.

There is a better way.

Lead Always. Leave Managing Behind.

To keep this personal, outside of these first few introductory pages, you won't find the words "manage" or "management" in this book except when referencing other sources. This is for two reasons.

The first and foremost one is because managing people sets the image of them as resources made of time and muscle. And that is not how a serving leader sees her or his people.

Secondly, the words "manage" and "management" are overused and therefore poorly understood. I frequently ask leadership teams how they'd define "manager" at a fifth-grade career day. They can't though – not without also using words and terms like "boss," "leader," "supervisor," or "the one in charge." For that matter, they can't define "manage" either.

At that, I'll joke that I "managed" to pass calculus... Does that make me a manager?

But don't think that I'm throwing aside the necessary and valuable disciplines that have come to be clumped into our overused M-word. The IDEAL approach incorporates the classic bodies of knowledge, phases and stages recommended by prominent project management sources. It's just that the IDEAL approach recasts those principles and techniques to help you, the leader, enable joy while simultaneously engaging excellence.

The IDEAL approach is calling you to LEAD.

Achieving truly excellent outcomes, not just satisfactory or compliant outputs, takes more than bookkeeping, contract tending and lots of nagging. Delivering a product that contributes delight to a customer and creates fulfilment for the team requires a leader who is willing, ready, able and persistent to – first and foremost – enable joy in the process. For everyone involved. That joy is an ingredient that will serve as the force multiplier you need to transform talents and engage excellence.

For the record, the underlying principles to this idea aren't new. Others have approached it before, just with varying conclusions. In his book *Winning at New Products*, Robert Cooper makes the case for both a clearly identified team leader and a project manager if an endeavor involves pursuing a new or innovative goal. Moreover, he describes the manager position as an "administrative and less entrepreneurial role."[1]

In other words, the IDEAL approach keeps people – not spreadsheets,

---

[1] Cooper, Robert G. *Winning at New Products*, p. 84.

budgets, schedules, checklists, and agendas – as the focusing power to ideally transform ideas into realities.

IDEAL – Based on Underlying Truths and Proven Practices

You may wonder how I came upon this IDEAL approach to leading a project. It's true that I've led projects myself. But if I were to base a whole book on how great I was, that should make you suspicious. Basing advice on one's personal experience alone is a tough vantage point, as we tend to rationalize how all our actions were somehow good... even if they were far from it.

Thankfully, I've had the privilege of spending several decades working alongside many project team leaders. I've gotten to talk with their people about their places in the process. And so I started to piece together what was different from project experiences that enticed them to want to do it again – and what drove them to run as far away as possible from the work and those in charge of that work.

What I heard from these people was more about the relationships involved than the spreadsheets. The stories were more about trust and distrust than about know-how and incompetence. Likewise, the desires were more about how well they felt aligned with priorities and connected with purpose than about how well they were informed of schedules and budgets.

Another key insight came from a study I initiated that looked across nearly 100 improvement projects at a large industrial complex. At the time, there was a belief that projects failed due to not following a prescribed, rational regimen; and, conversely, they only succeeded when the regimen was maintained.

Yet the study showed that following a regimen wasn't correlated to success and that not following it wasn't correlated to failure. This took the folks who deemed managing as the end all answer by surprise.

What the results basically pointed to was that success and failure were NOT correlated to good or poor management, or good or poor control. What the study did lead us to discover was that successful efforts were always accompanied by a feeling of purpose, a capability to create value and the belief that the project would be put to valuable use instead of dying in some three-ring binder report.

These three components alone do no guarantee success, but success was never achieved without these components of connect, create and contribute.

Looking across all that project experience, from leading to coaching to studying, I came to realize an underlying constant. For a project to be truly successful, in the eyes of the customers, team members and supporting contractors, the approach relied on something beyond the rational stuff about minding cost, schedule, scope, quality. It went beyond being good risk assessors or clever procurement agents. While those elements were necessary, they weren't the critical ingredients.

The project path to excellence is only partially paved with the rational tools of project "management." The path to an ideal project, must be equally paved with enabling joy and engaging excellence.

It's personal.

Personal – Challenge What You Believe About Project-Leading Habits

Now here's the tough part. If you want to be that personal leader you strive to be, you're going to have to examine your habits. To lead the IDEAL project, you'll need to look at your current way of doing things and the rationales behind them. In so doing, some of you may find that the IDEAL approach challenges you to change every aspect of leading a project. Others may find just a few aspects to refine.

Regardless, like any other kind of improvement you want to master, achieving this goal requires you to assess what you're doing now, challenge your beliefs and rationale, and then make the effort to believe, know and act on what you intend to change.

This is where a coach can be very valuable. He or she will act as an objective yet constructive mirror of your actions, your beliefs and your intentions. I'd venture so far as to say that a coach is a key – if not *the* key – enabler for your growth.

My desire for you is to become confident in the storyboard and components necessary for an IDEAL project so that you'll be ready to enable joy for those you lead and to engage excellence for your project.

To that end, this book is designed to be a combination guide, map, story and journal. Again, it's best enacted with a coach so that you can have that trusted mirror reflect back to you as you progress. It's also best enacted when you own it, personalizing it as necessary. This book does describe the overarching IDEAL approach, but that doesn't make you a passive participant by any means.

Prepare to be involved.

Your journey to IDEAL success will pursue two complementary goals.

1. To help you make intentional choices to *enable the people on your team to have joy in work.* When the project is all said and done, they'll look back and be grateful for how they not only helped fulfill the project but were fulfilled by the experience too.

2. To help you *engage excellence into the entire epic of a project.* It is framed in the context of a leader who is passionate about delighting the customer, while also being one who conducts the project as a collaborative promise to excellently transform an idea into a reality.

At the end of each section, there's a set of questions. These are your gateways to think it through and make it yours. Sure, you could just read this book. That wouldn't take long. And my guess is that you'd nod your head up and down in agreement with the topics, tools and theories for whatever span of time it took.

But glancing over these elements and components won't challenge you to relinquish the non-ideal habits that are holding you back. You need to make each part personal. Only then will you have truly prepared to direct your own epic endeavor to transform idea to reality.

For instance, the first section – **Why Joy** – provides many perspectives on what makes joy such an essential component in this equation. After you've read them, it's your turn. Why would YOU choose joy?

That critical thinking prompt is followed by **Your IDEAL Epic Storyboard**, where you will see how projects are like archetypical stories. By knowing this, you won't just be a project puppet. Rather you'll anticipate so as to respond, not react, to unfolding events. As leader, you'll be the director of that story. And by enabling joy and engaging for excellence, that narrative will become an epic adventure of how your team will transform an idea into a reality worth talking about.

The next three chapters explain the components of the storyboard. Respectively, they're **Enabling Joy, Engaging Excellence, and The Joy-Excellence Bond: Communication.** You should think of this section as explaining the parts and pieces of what you're doing, similar to when you open a new boardgame and check out the overall rules, the board itself, the sequence of play and the objectives.

The largest section of this book is **The IDEAL Approach**, which walks you through the act of moving from an idea to a real accomplishment, both in building your team and accomplishing that's team's goals. Each juncture of the approach has three elements. As you learn these, you will have the opportunity to 'make it yours,' so as to leverage the IDEAL approach to your own project.

Last but not least, I give you some guidance on the various tools and techniques via **The Toolbox** section**.**

This book is a complement to another book I authored, *Enabling Joy: Your Calling as a Leader.* That's a story that helps you understand how various personalities unpack what it means to enable joy – personally and professionally – and it's a great way to see how this worthwhile journey you're about to set out on could play out.

You can purchase it on Amazon in both Kindle and print copies. Until then though, let's get started and see what remarkable realities we can create as a result.

Let's go forth and make this personal!

"Anyone can manage consistency. Anyone can tell someone to repeat a process." Her hands went out of their own accord. *"But when there's some change being put in place, people are going to be more attuned to what we as leaders point to, what we focus on and what we say. So this time of change is the real test of whether we're doing our jobs as leaders."*

– From <u>*Enabling Joy*</u>

Why Joy

Why would you, a competent, busy leader of a critical project, care about enabling joy? What is it really going to do for you? Isn't "project management" about getting it done on time, on budget, and compliant to the specifications?

This book is for those of you who realize that, as a leader of a project team, you *want to do more than just meet the requirements*. You may want to create a wow for the customer or enrich the lives of those working on this project. Or perhaps you want to help people pursue a passionate purpose. Regardless, it's not about just fulfilling the terms of a contract.

If you can relate to all of that except for the "joy" term, don't worry. I understand why.

The reality is that you can get what looks like satisfactory results with good old-fashioned bully leadership. Yes, using fear will get you compliance; lots of project robots doing what they are told. And that can be confused with what others call successful project management.

But this only works in the short term. Besides the obvious problems involved, leaders who rely on the 'my way or the highway' approach can't sustain those good results. Since a cowering team leaves all decisions in the hands of the bully-leader, members only provide risk-free, non-creative answers and only do what they are told. And this becomes exhausting and exasperating. There are few things worse in a workplace than an exasperated, exhausted bully-leader making everyone else's lives miserable.

Enabling joy is the opposite of all that. It's the act of removing fear and instilling excitement. It's the way to sustain and grow your team's ability to transform their talents into strengths and to be engaged for excellence.

What you'll see is that joy isn't something that follows success. Joy is an ingredient that leads to success: to deep success that's perhaps better described as personal contentment and professional fulfillment. If you picture joy as a bunch of people celebrating a goal, think again. We need to give you a new image.

Joy is a human capacity, not an emotion.

Therefore, enabling joy is about unleashing the depth and breadth of that human potential.

The fundamental basis of why enabling joy is a proven part of effective leadership is found in the most well-read love story of all time. We won't cover that, but we will show how enabling joy is supported by world-class business gurus such as W. Edwards Deming, Noriaki Kano and Frederick Herzberg from the old school; and Shawn Achor, Daniel Kahnemann and Simon Sinek from the new school.

According to them, there's no way avoiding it. So let's get started finding out more about joy.

A Quick Preview: Enabling Joy

"Joy in work is when leaders 1) help us connect with the purpose and people, 2) create something of value for them or that purpose, and then 3) contribute that value – to put it into action."

This time, Dayzie nodded in agreement. "I see that. I mean, let's face it: One of our biggest fears is being alone or not connected. We're not sled dogs; we have an inner drive to have a purpose, or, as you put it, to create value and make a difference with that value."

– From <u>Enabling Joy</u>

Fundamentally, enabling joy is composed of three elements that the leader needs to bring to reality for the team.

First, there is a need to **connect**. Each team member must feel and believe he or she is connected to the team and the purpose and vision of the project.

Second, there is a need to enable each member to **create** value. Each team member has to understand and be equipped to create value for the team and toward the purpose of the project. Irrelevance is a leading cause for disengagement.

Third, there is a need to open the path so that each member knows that the value he or she creates can and will **contribute** to the team's purpose. If you want to disillusion and rob the joy of any job, take a person's good work and bury it under bureaucracy.

These three components of enabling joy will be explored in depth in the chapter on Enabling Joy. But let's first get a better understanding of what joy is and why we want to enable it.

Joy vs. Pleasure (the Dual Faces of Happiness)

"Joy is strength."

That is a quote from Mother Teresa, the Noble-laureate diminutive nun whose work in the slums of Calcutta got the attention of the United Nations and the United States Congress. Her words are a good premise to start from. They help us to realize that the joy we're enabling isn't some fleeting emotion. It's something much more powerful than that.

Joy, happiness and pleasure are three terms that often get confused. Yet they're not synonymous. Happiness, for one, is an emotion that can either be fleeting or sustained. When fleeting, it's reliant on external events, ushering in pleasure.

Sustained happiness, however, may be better defined as contentment. It's based on being at peace with our humanity and grateful for those external results that are the fruit of joy: of connecting, creating and contributing.

Here are a few examples:

Joy happiness is saving $1M through good work and financial stewardship.
Pleasure happiness is winning the lottery.

Joy happiness is cooking and serving a fine meal.
Pleasure happiness is eating a meal.

Joy happiness is being engaged in what we do.
Pleasure happiness is vacating (vacationing) from what we do.

Note that joy happiness creates and contributes. It develops strength. It is a fruit of discipline. Pleasure happiness, on the other hand, relies on external events. It is passive. And it is the fruit of obtaining temporary satisfaction.

Physiology *AND* Psychology

Here's another way of looking at it: Joy happiness is physiological, not just psychological.

We humans are endowed with amazing brains. To simplify talking about this complex organ, we're going to use some terminology from Daniel Kahnemann's prize winning book, *Thinking Fast and Slow*. We'll also be adapting ideas from Simon Sinek[2] from his talks on *Start With Why*.

They both refer to what may be called our two brains. One is what some call the old brain, or our reptile brain. In Kahnemann's terms, that's the fast brain, designed for quick decisions in an energy efficient way. It's the limbic

---

[2] For more information on Simon Sinek, refer to https://simonsinek.com.

system, the amygdala… that part of our brain that's about the size of a walnut and nestled deep down inside so that it's attached to our spinal cord.

The other is what some call the new brain, or the neo-cortex. It's designed for complex thinking, simulating scenarios, and making sense of unusual data. Kahnemann calls this thinking "slow," though it requires a whole lot of energy (think glucose) to do its thing.

As project team leaders, we are leading change by motivating a team to transform an idea into a reality and a customer desire into a customer delight. Our team therefore needs to be putting that glucose-gobbling neo-cortex to work so we can see a vision of the future. We need to understand that what we're doing today will create part of that vision. And we need to realize that what we contribute in said project is in some way part of our personal legacy.

This is hard when our natural inclination is to use that old brain. After all, it's fast and cheap as it looks for immediate rewards. Its best tools are instant analysis on whether to opt for fight, flight or freeze. Clearly then, the limbic brain is handy for dealing with survival. But the neo-cortex brain is where we can unleash the real power and strength of the human intellect.

It's where we can thrive.

Joy relies on the slow brain; pleasure teases the fast brain. That's why eating a salty and sweet snack is easy pleasure, while sustainable healthy eating requires strong decision making.

And there are few forces on earth that are stronger than joy.

A Curmudgeon's View

Interestingly, the early champion of enabling joy in work was W. Edwards Deming, who was frequently called the curmudgeon of quality. He's the guru that Japan credits with helping them out of their post-war starvation to become the industrial power they are today.

Deming preached his philosophy there first and then in the United States. With a career that spanned seven decades, he continued to work until he was 93 years old. It's interesting that this statistics-minded electrical engineer with a doctorate in mathematical physics spent his last decade emphasizing the need to enable joy in work.

Wait a minute though, you might be thinking. A curmudgeon preaching "joy?"

Yet the easy and accurate answer is yes.

In his later years, from about 1988 onward, Deming started his famous seminars by asking, "Why are we here?" He'd then answer his own question by stating that we're here to come alive, have fun and have joy in work.

When asked about how to develop a climate for innovation, Deming advised listeners to "concentrate on generating joy in work." That "the power of intrinsic motivation will lead to innovation." And while advising leaders and managers, he summed up their job by stating that the aim of management is to enable everybody to enjoy his work.[3]

To take the words from the curmudgeon himself: "Joy on the job comes not so much from the result – the product – but from the contribution to optimization of the system in which everybody wins."[4]

Joy = Customer Delight

Noriaki Kano developed a model that illustrates that, when serving customer needs, there are two possible results. One is necessary; the other is important.

Satisfaction is necessary.

Delight is important.

When we answer a request and give the customer what he or she asked for (i.e., what was bought), we satisfy him or her. And that might seem sufficient, particularly considering how many corporations have customer "satisfaction" as their goal. After all, in project life, there are so many dynamics that affect the ability to deliver the agreed-upon scope at the promised cost, schedule, and quality, that satisfying the customer is already a lofty goal.

But is satisfaction all there is?

Kano says no. He suggests we should strive to delight our client as well. The key insight of his model is that he differentiates satisfaction from delight

---

[3] Adapted from Henry Neave's *The Deming Dimension.*
[4] From W. Edwards Deming, *The New Economics.*

similarly to Herzberg's[5] theory of motivation, wherein Herzberg differentiates between motivators and "dis-satisfiers."

Kano contends that delight is something different than super satisfaction since it triggers excitement. In a project context, it means that customer delight goes beyond thinking that project excellence is measured solely by the time, cost, scope and schedule metrics. (More on this later and in the Toolbox)

In his book *The Excellence Dividend*, Tom Peters asks business leaders this question: Would you rather stay in a hotel where management has customer satisfaction as a top goal or in one where employees love their work? Most of us answer the latter because we know that, when employees are happy – even, say, joyful – we know that not only will the bathrooms and bedrooms be sparkling… Interactions with the staff will sparkle as well.

That's why a team whose leader fully enables joy equips it to not only satisfy customers but to delight them too.

Or, put another way, we want to enable joy because joy-enabled workers delight customers.

Joy's Opposite

A good way to understand any concept is to also understand its opposite. The opposite of joy is not unhappiness or sadness though. It's fear.

The easy way to make sense of this is to understand that a primary component of joy is connection. Meanwhile, one of humanity's biggest fears is being alone, which boils down to being without connection.

Our other fears? Having no purpose: no need or opportunity to create or contribute.

Understanding that joy's opposite is fear is key to understanding why extrinsic motivators (e.g., pay, benefits, job title, job security, workplace amenities, bonuses, etc.) are not really motivators at all, but controllers. They answer the basic needs of sustenance, shelter and security. By holding them out as incentives, we're essentially doing carrot-and-stick control. In which case, we're not leading at all; we're relying on the fear associated with not having

---

[5] Based on Frederick Herzberg's famous article in *Harvard Business Review*, "One More Time: How Do You Motivate Employees?"

sustenance, shelter or security.

This is why Herzberg humorously nicknamed these factors KITA[6], which stands for kick in the… pants. In employing them, we're doing much the same as old-fashioned dog trainers. No matter how much we succeed in deluding ourselves, all we're really doing is triggering the backend of the fear response.

For Deming's part, he always talked about driving out fear, and he built on that message by telling leaders what to do: enable joy.

The Joy Advantage

The more we choose joy, the more we make this world a better place to live. That's the sentiment Shawn Achor, author of *The Happiness Advantage*, gives us, hinting at the various levels of happiness, including the deepest kind, which is joy.

> *"How do the scientists define happiness? Essentially, as the experience of positive emotions -- pleasure combined with deeper feelings of meaning and purpose. Happiness implies a positive mood in the present and a positive outlook for the future.*

> *"Martin Seligman, the pioneer in positive psychology, has broken it down into three measurable components: pleasure, engagement and meaning. His studies have confirmed (though most of us know this intuitively) that people who pursue only pleasure experience only part of the benefits happiness can bring. While those who pursue all three routes lead the fullest lives.*

> *"Perhaps the most accurate term for happiness, then, is the one Aristotle used: eudaimonia, which translates not directly to 'happiness' but to 'human flourishing.' This definition really resonates with me because it acknowledges that happiness is not all about yellow smiley faces and rainbows.*

> *"For me, happiness is the joy we feel striving after our potential."[7]*

We're called to lead people in a way that establishes connections to other people and purpose, providing ways to help our teams create value and ultimately contribute that value in the pursuit of accomplishing our purpose.

---

[6] Reference to Frederick Herzberg's article in the *Harvard Business Review* article "One More Time: How Do You Motivate Employees?"

[7] From *The Happiness Advantage: How a Positive Brain Fuels Success in Work and Life* by Shawn Achor.

That's enabling joy.

Mother Theresa stated that joy is strength; the academics at Harvard found out why. Summed up, as we've already mentioned… while pleasure follows an event, joy precedes success. It causes it.

And that's why joy is strength.

> *"Study after study shows that happiness precedes important outcomes and indicators of thriving. In short, based on the wealth of data they compiled, they found that happiness causes success and achievement, not the opposite."*[8]

The Meaningfulness of Joy vs. the Joy in Meaningfulness

Are you still somewhat unconvinced that your job as a leader is to enable joy? Some of you may be thinking that leading is not about enabling joy. That it's about providing meaningfulness.

In which case, you're not alone.

Most of us perceive meaningfulness as something that is lasting. I agree with that definition. But I'd take it a step further and say it's still very similar to what we called sustained happiness or contentment earlier. Roy Baumeister has led some enlightening studies about meaningfulness and happiness. Looking at the results of his studies actually sheds light on why joy is as a precursor to having meaning.[9]

He found that connection is important for both meaning and sustained happiness. Contribution is important for meaning, yes, but that meaningfulness only comes from contributing to other people. Conversely, happiness comes from what they contribute to you. In other words, happiness is about getting what you want; meaningfulness is more about doing things that express yourself in serving others.

It's worth pointing out exactly how the studies peeled open this finding. Baumeister's researchers asked people if they were givers or takers. (Naturally, most of us don't want to admit to being takers, even though that's how so many

---

[8] Ibid.

[9] For details on Roy Baumeister's study, see https://aeon.co/essays/what-is-better-a-happy-life-or-a-meaningful-one and the online Harvard Business Review article found at https://hbr.org/2019/07/why-you-should-stop-trying-to-be-happy-at-work.

of us operate.) The results showed that takers experience more happiness but less meaning than their giver counterparts. Note that this happiness is the pleasure kind we talked about earlier, not sustained happiness or contentment.

This is fascinating. Baumeister's findings seem to affirm two bases for joy. One: The results affirm Deming's belief that joy in work is based not on the results but on the contribution. Second, his findings that meaningfulness comes from giving and happiness from taking is consistent with Herzberg's concept of "dis-satisfiers." Remember that "dis-satisfiers" are what people "take" from the job, like pay, benefits, etc. Even though those all provide happiness, they don't provide sustained happiness. On the other hand, Herzberg's "motivators" are based on helping people engage with and contribute to the job.

Now let's apply this for you, the project leader. The good news is that a project should be meaningful by nature. It's an effort that transforms an idea into a reality that can be contributed to its stakeholders. However, transforming that idea into reality is fraught with many complex and difficult challenges. The project epic will cause stress, worry, and differences of opinions. Those are not associated with happiness. Obviously. According to Baumeister, those are actually factors that lower happiness. Which also shouldn't come as a surprise. Yet Baumeister discovered that meaningfulness brings with it these very unhappy elements of reflecting on challenges, worry, disagreement, and stress.

In a strange way, this is good news for you, the project leader. By balancing enabling joy with engaging excellence, you have a path – an approach – to connect your team to their role in creating and contributing value while navigating the difficult challenges of the project work. With the IDEAL approach, you will be providing meaningfulness. That meaningfulness will be more lasting, more powerful than transient happiness. It will be yet another fruit of enabling joy.

It's why joy is strength.

Your Choice

Leading an IDEAL project requires enabling team joy and engaging work excellence. This starts with you.

As we've said before, **this is personal.**

So how about it? Are you all in? Are you onboard? Are you ready to commit? This is your crucible moment.

To help you answer this calling:

- Be ready to **challenge all your assumptions** about what it means to lead a project. Cease to be satisfied with just a project.

- **Think it through and make it yours**. Each of the chapters in this book have questions at the end to help you make it personal. They're your opportunity to think these ideas over, to challenge them and to compare them to what you believe. *Like a champion skier preparing her mind before a critical downhill event, use these reflective questions to engage your intuition. To picture the realities of your project. And then to exercise your mind so you can be better prepared to enable joy on the team and excellence in the work.*

- **Enlist the help of a coach**. Meeting with or telephoning a coach every few days – maybe once a week – to go over the questions with YOUR answers will provide accountability and feedback. No matter how experienced you are, having a coach will significantly increase your ability to IDEAL-ly lead your project. *Note: We'd recommend that your coach not be someone who is up or down your organizational chain of command.*

- Remember that transforming an idea into a reality is an ever-changing process. **Leaders lead change**.

Think It Through. Make It YOURS

1. Think about your personal reasons for accepting this role to lead the project. What is your primary motivation? To serve the customer? To serve the team? To serve your boss and/or organization? To serve yourself and your career?

2. Compare the descriptions of joy:
    *   Strength (Mother Theresa)
    *   Striving for our potential, human flourishing (Achor and Aristotle)
    *   The cause (not result) of success (Achor and Harvard study)
    *   The absence of fear (W. Edwards Deming)
    *   A push for meaningfulness (Baumeister).

    Which one do you most resonate with?

    Is there one you least understand or agree with? Why?

3. From the list below, which cause pleasure and which enable joy?
    *   Giving everyone Friday afternoon off
    *   Asking team members to have a heart to heart to resolve differences
    *   Bringing donuts to a boring meeting
    *   Conducting a meeting differently to increase participation and productivity
    *   Coming to grips with how to meet a demanding schedule
    *   Giving out bonuses
    *   Coming up with a way to save the customer money

4. List three actions you could do as a leader to enable joy.

5. Using extrinsic motivators – such as dangling carrots (e.g. money, benefits) or threatening with a stick (e.g. poor performance ratings) – can be addictive behavior. Why would that be?

   Think of other addictions that have short-term rewards but at long-term cost. Are these about pleasure or joy?

6. Think back to a time when you had a positive experience at a volunteer undertaking. Without the usual carrots and sticks to achieve desired behavior, how did the leaders enable joy?

7. We all like being the hero, but that isn't what enabling joy is about. Hero-leaders frequently get frustrated with their non-hero team, and then they devolve into being bully-leaders with a "do it or else" attitude and "my or the highway" tone.
   How are you ready to step away from the "hero" role?

8. As project lead, you're like the captain of a ship. If the ship runs aground, no matter who's on the bridge, the captain is accountable.

    Are you ready to accept accountability for the actions of your team? Are you apt to always blame poor team members, the changing situation, the irrational customer demands, the over-stringent regulations, etc. when situations "run aground"?

9. Deming once stated that 90% of the results you see are due to the system. As a project leader, you'll own much of that.

    When things go wrong for us, let's face it: We tend to blame the system. But when others have things go wrong, we tend to blame them personally. Like when we're late for work, we blame the traffic. When others are late however, we blame them personally.

    This is common. It's called the fundamental attribution error. Yet as the project leader, you need to realize that most of what goes wrong isn't due to personal reasons but the system YOU put in place.

    Are you ready to accept accountability for that?

10. How do you lead yourself? Do you say, "I have to…" or "I choose to…"? *[e.g. When you got up this morning, did you think "I have to go to work," "I get to go to work" or "I choose to go to work."]*

11. How do you lead in realms that are outside the business world? Think about how you lead your family or a volunteer activity: by fear or somehow else?

Your IDEAL Epic Storyboard

We don't live in a photograph. We live in a story. A movie. Our lives are a steady roller coaster ride of twists and turns of plot and a constant unveiling of characters and relationships. And while we may not readily see the heroes or villains as clearly as in a theater, we do have them.

When we go to the movies, we're entertained by the dynamics of human interaction: that ebb and flow of relationships and the back and forth of good versus evil. Isn't that why we go in the first place?

While we may like all that action and drama on the big screen though, oddly enough, we're not really all that fond of the same suspense and tension in real life.

You, as leader of a project team are off to accomplish transforming an idea into a reality: to conquer the enemies of Not Enough Time and Money by pulling together a team of folks to tackle it... even if they are still wondering how they'll produce this daunting project.

That is backdrop of your project movie. As the leader, you'll produce, direct and own much of the way your team's movie plays out. Don't you want to make that movie epic?

But before you fret too much that you didn't expect to find yourself in the movie business, we have some reassuring news. Movies attempts to replicate real life. Your project *is* real life. Now let's prepare for the real life of a project.

Since projects, by design, have a defined beginning and a defined end, the project experience – with its ad hoc cast of players and transformation of an idea into reality – is very similar to our typical drama or movie experience. So, like any good story, your project has a plot.

Actually, your project will contain two archetypical plots.

First, you have the dynamics of a team coming together. It will look a lot like the plot line of a romantic comedy, where guy meets girl, they have an initial spark, something goes wrong and they hate each other, they resolve the issue, they live happily ever after.

Then you have the excitement of how a team actually takes on an objective that seems insurmountable: budgets and schedules that are ridiculously tight. The arduous planning and plotting. The handwringing of what could go wrong. The late hitch in the plans. The recovery, daring execution and well-played adaption to surprises. And then the celebration of a success.

That, as you can see, looks lot like the plot line of an action movie.

With that said, every action movie or romcom is unique despite following the same archetypical plot lines. They each have contextual components: elements that keep them from becoming copyright lawsuits. Here's how yours should look on paper and in practice alike…

For the team to work together, you will lead by enabling joy. As mentioned before, that's comprised of connecting, creating and contributing. (I'll unpack these further in the next chapter.) Meanwhile, for project excellence to be achieved, you'll lead by:

- Tending to the rational aspects of cost, schedule, scope, quality
- Caring about the relational aspects of building your in-house team
- Inviting contractors to join the effort
- Respecting the input from stakeholders
- Ensuring supplies are provided and risks are mitigated.

The final contextual component is essentially what holds most great dramas together: the ebb and flow of communication. Your project success will hinge on how well you bind together the interactive and administrative aspects of the project. This combination will ride on how well you lead and direct the communication that's the glue of project success.

That's it. The romance and adventure of your project is a given. It's only how epic your project will be that's up in the air, and that is largely dependent on your leadership in producing and directing that drama.

To help you, we first take a closer look at what's behind those plot flows and the components of team joy and project excellence.

The Team Dynamics

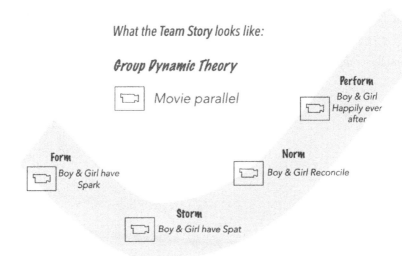

What the *Team Story* looks like:

Group Dynamic Theory

Movie parallel

Perform
Boy & Girl Happily ever after

Form
Boy & Girl have Spark

Norm
Boy & Girl Reconcile

Storm
Boy & Girl have Spat

There's a classic little rhyme about the phases of team dynamics that's been around for decades. It's easy to remember and surprisingly predictive: Form, Storm, Norm, Perform. Here's how each plays out.

- **Form**: "Hey, how you doing? Glad you're here."
  When we build a collective identity and understand each other, we generate an appreciation of why we're all here in the first place.
- **Storm**: "Uh-oh… Jack and Jill are at odds about this."
  It's practically inevitable that we'll experience those awkward and tense moments as we iron out our differences.
- **Norm**: "We're hitting our stride now!"
  We start generating team alignment, capitalizing on different talents and perspectives, fulfilling our roles and co-creating the value.
- **Perform**: "This is good; let's go for great!"
  We're continually improving and innovating, using data, assessments

and feedback to improve performance instead of getting defensive.

Notice that, graphically, Form-Storm-Norm-Perform is like a roller coaster, with Storm being like the valley of despair, and Perform being so much better than before we had a team.

Let's relate this to an archetypical romance plot.

- **Form:** Guy meets girl. There's a spark of ooh-la-la.
- **Storm:** One of them does something that makes the other storm away.
- **Norm:** Someone makes a turnaround, the other accepts/forgives, and things are looking almost normal.
- **Perform:** Guy and girl are joyfully ooh-la-la all over again.

The Work Dynamics

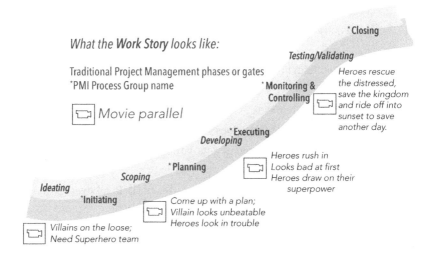

What the **Work Story** looks like:

Traditional Project Management phases or gates
*PMI Process Group name

Movie parallel

* Closing

Testing/Validating

Heroes rescue the distressed, save the kingdom and ride off into sunset to save another day.

* Monitoring & Controlling

* Executing
Developing

* Planning

Scoping

Ideating

* Initiating

Villains on the loose; Need Superhero team

Come up with a plan; Villain looks unbeatable Heroes look in trouble

Heroes rush in Looks bad at first Heroes draw on their superpower

A project is achieved along a process. The graphic shows a classic S-shaped curve (a slightly flat S, but still an S) that depicts a somewhat controlled start with slowly growing activity across time. As designs mature, plans take shape and more is accomplished as the idea becomes reality through building or writing or coding. As the physical reality comes to its conclusion, the amount of work tapers back off as the testing and validating ends, and the project is officially completed.

The Project Management Institute, or PMI, has defined five process groups that describe this overall process: Initiating, Planning, Executing, Monitoring & Controlling, and finally, Closing. The dynamic, ad-hoc nature of projects has given rise to overarching macro processes like the Stage-Gate®[10] Model.

---

[10] *Stage-Gate®* is a trademark of Stage-Gate International Inc. in the United States and Australia, and of R. G. Cooper and Associates Inc. in Canada. In EU, the trademark is held by R. G. Cooper.

Stage-Gate® isn't another type of project management. Instead, it supplements project management methods, providing a way to define project stages that pre-define what the team will deliver at the end of each, i.e. a "gate," that has clear criteria for continuing or ceasing.

To define our project lifecycle, we'll use these terms:

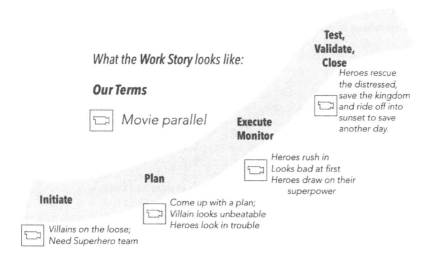

- **Initiating** – That phase of getting the project approved, funded and sponsored; and pulling together a project team.

- **Planning** – The phase wherein all the schedule, cash flow, risk mitigations, sources of contractors and supplies, and stakeholder concerns are put on paper and a design is developed on how to pull the job off.

- **Executing and Monitoring** – This is where the action happens: where buildings get built, software gets created, campaigns are conducted, etc. It's the part where we make sure we're committing to our plans. And that, when those plans don't pan out, we have recovery actions put quickly in place.

- **Testing, Validating, and Closing** – This is where we sign off on the test documents and certifications, hand over the keys and receive final payments.

Let's now look at how this project workflow and our archetypical action movie plots are analogous. To reinforce that projects are team events, let's only consider action movies with a team of heroes. That will also get us out of having to explain that lonely dark side, which heroes always seems to have.

- **Initiating:** The team learns of a need because some megalomaniac genius is off doing mischief – and they decide to *do* something!

- **Planning:** The team develops a plan that looks great at first, until there's a hitch, making them argue about petty differences. The heroes' plans waffle between looking hopeless and hopeful.

- **Executing and Monitoring:** The hero team rushes in according to their plan to transform their rescue idea into a rescue reality, ousting the villain and changing the world or humbling the megalomaniac. Invariably, in the process, there are unplanned surprises. Or they run out of some resource. Or the villain is "dastardlier" than expected. Sometimes, in order to get past those problems, they'll rely on some backup or support or new friend. But, through it all, our heroes do what heroes do. They never give up, and they vanquish the villains. They achieve victory.

- **Testing, Validating, and Closing** – The heroes the rescue the imperiled, restoring order and making ready for a happily-ever-after scenario (or a sequel).

The Project Epic

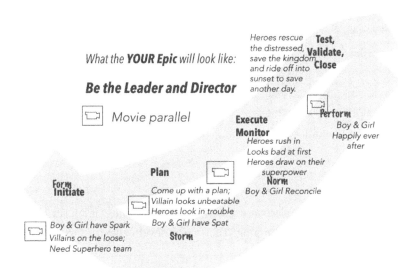

What the **YOUR Epic** will look like:

Be the Leader and Director

🎬 Movie parallel

Form
Initiate

Boy & Girl have Spark
Villains on the loose;
Need Superhero team

Plan

Come up with a plan;
Villain looks unbeatable
Heroes look in trouble
Boy & Girl have Spat

Storm

Execute
Monitor
Heroes rush in
Looks bad at first
Heroes draw on their
superpower
Norm
Boy & Girl Reconcile

Heroes rescue **Test,**
the distressed, **Validate,**
save the kingdom **Close**
and ride off into
sunset to save
another day.

Perform
Boy & Girl
Happily ever
after

Now let's pull this all together.

Remember: You will produce and direct both the team story AND the work story. TOGETHER. They're linked. Interrelated. And one will have an effect on the other.

IDEAL is the approach to script and direct these dual story lines so that, when they're all said and done, the team gets to live joyfully ever after. And, against all odds, the project is victoriously achieved with delighted customers.

While every project will be unique, there are some very common experiences of note. Very typically, as shown by the graphic above, project teams tend to get plunged into the storming phase with the type of work that happens in planning. That's easy to understand since that's the stage we're all comparing our assumptions for how to go about the hard work to complete the project.

It's a democratic sort of phase, and there will be just as many opinions as there are people on the team.

By and large, teams mature during planning thanks to the clarity of schedules and explicit roles, responsibilities and plans that mature into the norming – maybe even the performing – stage.

Of course, each project has its own personality, tempo and maturation. And it is possible for a team leader to be highly effective in the initiation phase of getting his or her team through storming and into norming. That would look like this.

When the Leader Enables Joy early in the project lifecycle –
The romance is at happily ever after while the heroes are still suiting up.

Conversely, it's possible that even with all the planning, the team never really matures through the storming. They never develop the trust to have the tough conversations.

But those tough conversations have to happen somewhere if you're to be at all successful as a project team. Sadly, that means the difficult storming will likely happen during the fast and furious execution phase. And that is hard!

Sometimes Enabling Joy is more of a roller coaster than originally anticipated;

But the IDEAL approach will get you where you need to be.

In that case, the story would look like this.

From here on in though, we'll simplify the explanations by assuming a typical case where planning ignites storming and nurtures a path to norming.

Think It Through. Make It YOURS

1. Recall a previous project you have been on. How could it have been a gripping movie?

2. What would be the enticing line on the poster or trailer about the movie of your project?

3. What are the current realities you see on your team that will probably cause that storm portion of team development?

Enabling Joy

Let's take a look at joy in real life. In the chapter "Why Joy," we unpacked what joy is – that it isn't a feeling. That joy is strength: an ingredient that brings forth the capacity of our human gifts. We learned that Aristotle talked about it being how we flourish, and Baumeister showed its relationship to having meaning.

We also learned that, as a leader, it's your role to enable joy. And that would seem to be a more difficult task. Deming was definitely on the right track when he evolved his advice from "drive out fear" into "enable joy." Yet I found those two words alone didn't fully help me at a person-to-person, situation-to-situation level.

What could I do to be intentional and purposeful in that goal?

The key is in the components of joy, as mentioned briefly in the first chapter. By understanding these components a bit more, we'll start to see how to enable joy, understanding how it's not about making people happy... and, yet, it does.

It starts with this picture. (In case you're wondering, I drew it myself.) This is a picture of enabled joy, and it's also a picture of joy.

Changing a diaper on a little one: It's not one of our favorite parenting duties. We're never hoping for a day when we'll have a lot of diapers to change. It is truly a stinky task.

Yet it serves as a perfect picture of what we're angling for nonetheless. When a parent changes a baby's diaper, he or she is able to connect with the purpose at hand and with the person.

That's a clue. Think about those who may be paid to change diapers. Do you think their attitude is somewhat different than a parent's?

Now think about exactly what a parent does when changing a diaper. She or he creates value: the value of going from wet and stinky to dry and clean. And who gets that value? The baby. The parent gives the value away: That's his or her contribution.

Now, as the person in charge of your project, you'll need to assign out a lot of diaper-changing types of jobs. You'll need them to be done right too. And in order to truly do that – to take the results from satisfactory to impressive – you'll need to intertwine engaging excellence with enabling joy.

Enabling joy is about making work meaningful, fulfilling and engaging. As we've said before, it's different than making work pleasurable. That's why this diaper-changing metaphor works well. Because, as we've also stated, diaper changing is a stinky job. There's no way around that.

Yet consider what the work really involves (no matter how removed this diaper changing metaphor may seem from your leadership role right now)…

- An intimate **connection between two people** and a clear **connection to the purpose** at hand

- Definitively **creating value,** transforming dissatisfaction into delight

- **Value that's able to be contributed** – in essence, given away

What does it mean to enable joy? It is when we lead so as to enable people to **connect, create and contribute**.

Let's unpack each of those three terms.

Connect

This is the *sine qua non* – the essential component – of enabling joy in work. The ability and willingness to connect is the underlying intrinsic motivation that leaders must promote.

As people, we need and long for connection to others. Studies[11] continually affirm that connectedness is a key factor in a long happy life, in mental health, and in organizational productivity.

We need to be connected. To others. To purpose. This means your job as a leader is to enable your people to be and stay connected to their colleagues and their goals.

More than likely, you're familiar with the statistic that shows how people typically leave their jobs due to some disconnect with their bosses or peers – and not because of pay, office size, or benefits. While it's true that those extrinsic components may play a supporting role in their workplace unhappiness, the initial driver to look elsewhere most of the time is a broken sense of connectedness.

---

[11] Studies include The Grant Study, a 75-year-long Harvard study on adult happiness led by Robert Waldinger, director of the Laboratory of Adult Development at Massachusetts General Hospital; and Project Aristotle, a Google teaming analysis performed in 2012.

We don't just need to be connected to our team though. We also need to be connected to our team's purpose. We long to connect to a purpose bigger than ourselves.

We all strive to have meaning in our lives – a purpose for our passion and our perspiration. Hundreds of books on managing and leading, despite their unique perspectives, still resonate on the value of creating a shared vision and common mission, complete with some compelling statement that aligns the purpose of why the organization exists and what its dreams are. While there's a lot of cynicism around vision and mission statements, much of which is well earned, there is a fundamental rightness to the concept. It's a matter of the leader being able to visibly promote the purpose and effectively communicate why it's more than just a catchy phrase. Why it's worth being connected to.

As a leader, you have a fundamental, critical role in taking people through this change called a project. What happens during times of change that makes leading, rather than just managing, so critical? Relationships, purposes and/or routines are modified and redirected. And each and any one of those factors can be excellent breeding grounds for team members to get or feel **disconnected**.

In short, what he or she could rely on yesterday might not be so reliable tomorrow. **Change necessitates a disconnection from the status quo, and that's why it's so important for leaders to promote connectedness to the new task at hand**.

As leaders then, it's your first priority to offer a steady stream of encouragement to refocus: a new shared vision that offers the same kind of connection in the end. When employees have to let go of their comfortable habits, they more than ever need to feel connected to what their new purpose is and to know that they're not alone.

Create

This is where the dream – the purpose we're connected to – transforms from idea to reality. It's where we transform raw input into valuable output.

The term "create" sometimes evokes a mental image of being creative, and many of us dismiss ourselves as being anything but that. We limit the definition to being artistic or musically inclined. And in so doing, we cheat ourselves at least a little bit.

The term "create" can and should encompass so much more than that. Consider the diaper example given before. We create a solution to a problem, comfort where there was distress, happiness where there was crying and freshness where there was stinkiness.

Deming, for one, had an elegantly simple definition for all work: what's become known as the SIPOC. The acronym stands for Suppliers Inputs Process Outputs Customers, and it's drawn out right below.

Supply	**I**nputs	**P**rocess (Transformation)	**O**utputs	**C**ustomer OutCome
Person/Organization that provides the raw goods	What is needed to enable the Process	Where the real value happens; transforming inputs into outputs	The tangible items that are produced	The end result and the desired value in the eyes of the customer

In essence, what it means is that all work should be defined as a process where inputs are transformed into outputs that are valued by customers. That transformation of inputs to outputs is the creative value at the core of what humans endeavor to do.

Therefore, another way to look at your role of enabling joy is to unleash that calling to create: that creative passion. That creative role.

Some of that role is administrative in nature, of course. It's assigning talents to tasks in a sensible way. But even most of that still boils down to helping each person see himself or herself as creating value: as being vital parts of the endeavor at hand. Like an orchestra conductor, we must enable each "musician" to collectively play together in creating our symphony.

Special Note:

The PMBOK® Guide, along with standards such as ISO 9000 and the Software Engineering Institute's Capability Maturity Model are based on a similar process approach, frequently described as Inputs, Tools and Techniques, and Outputs.

Contribute

Contribute. This verb is derived from Latin root words which, when combined, mean to bestow together or bring together. Looked at that way, it's not hard to see how it circles right back to the necessity of connecting.

To quote Deming, "Joy on the job comes not so much from the result, [or] the product, but from the contribution." This is where task becomes treasure.

Keep in mind that contributing is not the same as delivering, which typically entails the act of simply handing over, as in a package or correspondence. The word "contribute," meanwhile, implies giving of ourselves and seeing that gift appreciated.

In order to make it even more clear why this concept – this crucial mindset-driven behavior – is the third element necessary in enabling joy in work, consider when proper contribution doesn't occur. Think about those times when teams developed great ideas, great plans, great prototypes and great products… only to see the value they created get lost in bureaucratic red tape, die in the morass of political maneuvering, or just sit on a shelf as hostages to poorly balanced priorities, capital, time or courage.

Stop and really consider that for a second. It's a sobering thought. But it's one that should motivate you.

As a leader, you're the barrier buster. You're the one the others look to when it comes to providing the crucial link necessary to push the created value toward its contribution phase, and then to properly contribute that value to the customer, the users, the business, the society, and even the team itself in the form of learning, experience and righteous (not self righteous) pride.

It's critical for you, as a project leader, to deeply respect that component. Contributing isn't about delivering alone. It's about meaningfulness.

First off, recall that meaningfulness is related to being a giver. That contrasts it with being happy, which is related to taking. So the contribute component, the giver dimension, ensures that your project has an explicit and intentional meaningfulness.

Secondly, as Viktor Frankl shares in his book *Man's Search for Meaning*, life lacks meaning without purpose. Without contribution being evident, explicit and effective, the team doubts its collective purpose. And each individual member begins to question the meaningfulness of their efforts on this project.

Meaningfulness also relies on efficacy – that all the actions in the Create component have made a positive contribution toward realizing our goals and values. That provides team members with the feedback and reinforcement to regard their effort in a positive light as a good and worthy endeavor.[12]

---

[12] Based on and adapted from Ralph Baumeister's essay The Meanings of Life, September 16, 2013.

Diaper changing.
Joy to the World.
Times of change.
Turning a crying baby into a happy one by first being able to connect person-
ally and with purpose.
Creating a smile and contentment for that little person.
Giving the value of that contentment away...
Joanna felt just a whisper of clarity about where these thoughts were heading.
The trail bent sharply upward, but it had already plunged back into the trees,
offering cooler air under the resulting canopy. Joanna knew from past experi-
ences that she was now near the last of the uphill portion, even if that fact was
hard to see from where she was right then. Still in pursuit of an actionable ex-
planation, she honed in on a new product one of the teams had worked on. The
designers and artisans who'd originally come up with the idea were all given
the proper respect during the subsequent building phases. And every other per-
son involved felt like they'd been a worthwhile part of the final product, a de-
vice that had delighted their customer and made Coeurs itself a lot of money.
The team had had a clear sense of purpose and a family-like tightness, two fac-
tors that had greatly aided it with this particular product. The device had come
about after a customer had made a seemingly impossible request. But this group
of men and women had hatched a plan, a design and a process to pull it off any-
way.
And then they'd followed through.
They had, in essence, changed the diaper.

– From <u>Enabling Joy</u>

Think It Through. Make It YOURS

1. Look back over the previous week. In those moments where you noticed a spark of interest or engagement from those whom you led, what was your action that prompted it? Was that action or communication something that enabled connection... the ability to create value... the access to contribute value more freely?

2. As a project leader, do you have direct control of the career or pay of those on your team?
   a. If you do, then how do you <u>not</u> allow that power to be the way you lead?

   b. If you don't, then how do you influence without that?

3. Can you see now how your role as a leader is to enable people to be truly human; or, as Aristotle says, "human flourishing?" Jot down one situation that you see a better joy-enabling way to lead someone through it.

Engaging Excellence

The IDEAL approach to engage excellence is about applying the helpful tools that move and track a project's progress from idea to reality so as to be in full concert with your calling to enable joy. Recall that enabling joy increases engagement. Now it's time to direct that engagement.

To engage excellence, you will lead three sets of components.

- The Rational Four – Cost, Schedule, Scope, Quality
- The Relational Three – In-House, Contractors, Stakeholders
- The Readiness Two – Suppliers, Risk

The IDEAL approach puts these typical project disciplines in a context that keeps at the forefront that your calling as leader is about engaging your team in an endeavor to transform an idea into a reality in a way that delights the customer.

The names for the sets of components are my own. I've found that most project M-word books clump all these nine together. This makes it seem like they're all of the same ilk. They're not. Some appeal to our need for logic, some to our social needs and some to our need to handle uncertainty. Explicitly acknowledging these differences helps you adapt how you need to train, supervise, monitor and assign how your team deploys these project achievement tools.

Let's take a fresh look at these necessities of project excellence.

The Rational Four

These might better be called the obvious four. They're the tangible elements of every project, monitored with an array of schedules, Gantt charts, spreadsheets, and status reports... the explicit dimensions of your project.

But that explicit nature shouldn't fool you into thinking they're the principal pillars of successful project completion. The tools used to monitor, control and predict these rational four components are well-established, so we won't dwell on them here. What we will do is look at them without the M-word. We'll instead view each as a leader who needs to engage excellence in these four dimensions – with enabling joy.

As we look into the future, we see a different approach for these Rational Four. Reports are out that artificial intelligence (AI) is becoming one of the new realities of running a project. It's already in use in areas of cost analysis, schedule analysis and contract analysis. So it's not an unforeseen possibility that the Rational Four may be done primarily in the confines of your computer, leaving you the work of leading what to do with that analysis as Project Leader.

Steward Cost

The project's funding is the tangible evidence of the trust that the customers (payers and users), are putting in our leadership. They're literally "showing you the money!"

This makes us the stewards of their financial investment in this project. As project leaders, we must be diligent to ensure we communicate clearly and consistently about the cost aspects of our project. And we should be transparent about the project's costs, comparing them to estimates and expectations, and being ready to explain the differences.

Note that this book isn't intended to be the how-to reference for cost control, cost profiles, cost at risk, earned value, or the plethora of other concepts that surround project financing and budgeting. But it is critical to highlight that a key part of project excellence is maintaining ownership and accountability of the stewardship of the financial aspects. Trust is fortified with transparency.

As project leaders, how the money is flowing in and out of the project is often a flammable topic. When team members miss an estimate, procure the wrong supplies or seem to run afoul of good fiscal sense, the resulting stress and anxiety frequently causes us to slip into bully-leaders: to "fix" the problem by reading them the riot act.

Yet to integrate engaging excellence with enabling joy, we must put these situations in the context of connecting, creating and contributing. There is no standard route, but here are the foundational steps:

1. Lead yourself. You have to avoid dipping back into your own storming phase. It's difficult to lead others well when we're struggling to exhibit good behavior in ourselves.

If the monetary missteps make your blood boil, then take a pause. Taking an hour to cool off and let yourself handle the issue as a caring leader will pay dividends later. Just like in an airplane, how they advise you to put your own air mask on before helping others, you'll find the same is true when facing project turbulence.

2. Lead others. When planning how to drive accountability, retrain and coach, you need to ask yourself: "Will the way I'm doing this increase their connectedness to purpose and people? Will it increase their ability to create value? Or just make them feel more shamed when they can't?"

Keep the Promise - Schedule

Time is a precious, non-returnable commodity. As leader, you and your team must fully recognize that you've been entrusted with this valuable, non-refundable asset of your customer's life.

In today's world, similar to cost, there's a plethora of tools to help you provide your customer, your team and yourself with a good look at how well you can maintain your promises in this way. It's just a matter of knowing them – before you set out.

Don't say you'll rebuild the temple in three days unless you have credible confidence in that promise. And when the vagaries of life put it at risk, waiting to see if it will get better is rarely a winning strategy. Continual honesty, even when facing setbacks, shows respect from you and your team.

As a leader, the best approach is to go to the source when estimating how long a job will take. What does that mean? It is based on the principle that those who do the work are at that best vantage point to estimate the time required. Estimating should be first based on estimated durations that then drives estimated completion dates.

This approach, to have the worker estimate duration, maintains a vital connection of the worker to the timeline of the project. Many times, tasks are assigned a timeframe because that's what's available. There are good reasons to do it that way, to be sure. But holding people accountable to a schedule-driven time versus work driven duration is problematic – the doer has very little connection to that externally derived promise.

People should be accountable to time estimates they create based on their knowledge of the work to be done. Holding your people accountable doesn't need to be punitive, but it should always result in those people being better engaged and better equipped. Making poor assumptions about how long a task takes can only be corrected when people are 1) accountable for their estimates and 2) willing to learn how to make better estimates.

Mind Scope

What is scope? Scope from the customer's perspective is their description of how the idea needs to be transformed into a reality. Their description of scope is in terms of the finished *product* – the "O" of the SIPOC model we mentioned earlier (also described in The Toolbox).

Scope, from your project team's perspective, is your *promise* of what will be transformed from idea to reality. Scope is typically defined in the words of a working agreement, be it a written contract or spoken words over a hand-shake. It may be a picture (such as an engineering or architectural drawing) or a list of features (as may be typical of a software project).

Regardless, for nearly all projects, it's a way to describe a desired future state: a real output in the future based on an idea today.

As with cost, the expectation is that you will use the typical scope control and monitoring tools that are well-established and found readily in any book on how to run a project. These tools will tell you *when* you need to act.

The IDEAL approach defines *how* you, as leader, need to act. But before you go ahead and try to implement this step, let's check on how you should be thinking as you go into it.

In the IDEAL approach, you will lead "minding scope." By this, I mean you'll consistently remember that the way people focus their energy and expend their time and place their priorities is based on how their minds see this scope. Hence your job as a leader is to "mind scope."

When scope deviations occur, they're the result of some fuzziness in your project team's "mind view" of that scope. Of the two possible deviations, one involves doing less than the customer is asking for, leaving scope unachieved. The other entails doing more than the customer is asking, resulting in value for which there will not be sponsorship or reimbursement.

In other words, your team went overboard for no good reason.

In either case, as a leader, you can reduce – maybe even altogether elimi-nate – these deviations going forward by looking at how your team discon-nected from the desires of the customer the first time it happens. Ask yourself these questions:

Is this a case where your project team, as subject matter experts, made a decision that assumed they knew better and that the customer would see as much later? Or did they think the additional value is a new necessity or new requirement? Is this a case where your project team thought the extra would delight the customer and that approval to pay for it would be a natural reaction by the sponsor?

In the case of underachieving, did your team see a way to satisfy an underlying need at a lower cost, or did they not understand the breadth or depth of what the customer wanted?

Underachieving and overachieving scope is easier to see in projects where the deliverable is tangible, like construction of a building. It's less tangible when the scope is a list of features, like building a database suite. And it's even more fluid in projects that produce campaigns.

Regardless of over or underachieving, the root actions you need to take as the project leader are about enabling joy. The scope control and monitoring tools, like S-curves, earned value, and such, have done their job. They've told you about the out-of-scope condition.

Yet pointing to those tools and telling your team to make it right is like yelling at a baseball batter and telling him to not strike out. It's obvious and pointless. You need to help your team "mind scope." You need to go back to enabling joy: back to reconnecting them to the shared purpose. The shared vision. The core values.

If something has gone wrong, your job is to go back to realigning the value to be created with the shared purpose. You need to reinforce the reality that the only value worth giving the customer is the one agreed to by the customer.

A caveat about Scope: When the stage is set for the project team and customer to be at odds with each other, it sets the stage for the completed project to be no better than the contractual scope. Sadly, this "at odds" condition is frequently initiated when the customer selected your team based on lowest cost. Chances are, when competing for low price, your project team sharpened the estimate to shave off any possible excess, with the expectation that these would be agreed upon later. The I and D junctures of the IDEAL approach will

LEAD THE **IDEAL** PROJECT • 57

be critical to building the needed trust to set the stage for that agreement.

Mind Scope: The tools will tell you *when* you need to lead. But enabling joy is *how* you'll lead.

Build in Quality

Quality isn't something you check when the job is over. It is built in from the start. It's a direct function of how well you as a leader have connected each team member and empowered them to truly create value and contribute.

When each team member is essentially owning and signing their work, they're less likely to be mindless drones you rent eight hours a day and more likely to be co-owners of the project at hand. This will promote the kind of discipline and diligence that are the foundations of continually building in quality in every step.

When you're having quality issues, the odds are that you're not enabling joy in work. That you have team members who are disconnected or unable to create value, or who believe their work doesn't matter. (For a deeper look at this, pay particular attention to the Flow model explained in the D juncture of The IDEAL Approach)

When your team is fully connected to purpose and people, they're ready to identify what is needed to meet that purpose, complete with trust in their team-mates to identify issues and problems.

Let's say some customer requirements appear outdated or irrelevant. Maybe some current requirements had evolved to eliminate problems that no longer exist. A team that has good connection to purpose and people will challenge those requirements, and/or suggest ways to meet the intent or to eliminate unnecessary cost to the customer. Without that connection, however, you have people who will follow the letter of the law, blindly compliant to the point of being detriments to the client and the company.

Quality is built all the way through. The IDEAL approach's elements continually link engaging excellence with enabling joy, thereby setting the will and the wherewithal for each project player to be continually an enable for quality, engaged in achieving that which will delight the customer.

"Notice how I said 'leading,' not 'managing.' We have all the numbers and graphs we need to assess work management. What we were lacking was a way to assess how well we lead people. And we now have a way to do that."

– From <u>Enabling Joy</u>

The Relational Three

The project is transforming an idea to reality. Only people have ideas. The project is accomplished by connected people creating value and contributing that value to the purpose. Only people can do that process.

Projects are not done by numbers on a spreadsheet, nor by bars on a Gantt chart, nor by S-curves or man-loading charts. They're accomplished with minds and muscles.

To lead the IDEAL project, you'll need to be a careful custodian of the talents entrusted to you. Those talents are found in your team, and that team is roughly composed of people from three different families.

The In-House Family

The first source is naturally your own organization. This is your corporate or department family. And like family, there are bonds and secrets that exist between you and your colleagues: a level of wanting to protect your own.

As the leader, you'll be tempted to treat family differently. Sometimes that's good; sometimes not. Regardless, you'll be susceptible to that same crazy behavior we see in parents in kids' sports, where they can be blind to the actual sporting ability their prodigy has. There's no magic formula, but as you'll see in The IDEAL Approach, you will need to pull this family together to be able to speak truth to each other.

Special Note on Matrix Management:

In its basic form, matrix management has the organization's talent set under functional leads (e.g., engineering, design, planning, sales, etc.) and the project work under program leads (e.g. product, platform). The money flows through the programs, and the work is done by the talent. So there's a built-in creative interdependence. Projects need talent; talent needs money.

In matrix management, while the talent reports to the functional manager per the organizational chart, they actually report to the project manager(s) for the work itself. This can sometimes cast the perception of the talent, though working for the same organization as the project leads, appear to the project leader as being more akin to contractors.

As project leader, you need to embrace that talent regardless. This is why the advice for contractors is to treat them like they're your own organization.

Everyone connected, creating and contributing to the project must be considered part of the same project family.

The Contractor Family

Project teams are frequently like a Noah's ark of creatures, with contractors coming in to help with aspects we're less-equipped to handle. This contractor family can range from talent that is expert at some intellectual aspect to talent that is expert at accomplishing routine work in an efficient manner.

Either way, these contractors bring a special challenge with them – they're part of your schedule but not in your corporate family. So they have competing priorities that your project – especially your project leadership – won't have control over. And getting them to be on your project when you need them to be isn't as straightforward as getting your own organization's people there.

How is a project leader to accomplish this? This aspect of project work is commonly called integration. It's the necessity of the corporate family members – the native project team members – to be open, welcoming and honest with those contractors. This can begin with a mentality shift: with the native team setting aside their prejudice that contractors somehow don't care as much.

The project leader needs to be intentional in this regard. Each contractor should be as connected to the purpose as the corporate family. They can't be treated as second-class citizens.

You're hiring them to create value and to contribute that to the project goals. And you must be explicit to set the connection.

The best metric of how well you're doing with interconnecting the various talents is when contractors become trusted problem solvers to problems you didn't know you had... or to ones your core team couldn't solve. That's reflective that they've been enabled to connect, create and contribute.

The Stakeholder Family

Stakeholders. That's a confusing term, I know. So here's a way to understand it. Stakes provide both the grounding and tension that hold up tent poles and therefore tents.

Your project tent needs stakeholders. They represent a collection of interests from bill-payers, to end-users to regulators. In a way, all of them could be called customers, so let's define each of those in turn...

- **Sponsor or Bill-Payer**: This is the party that's paying for the project and very frequently (though not always) the recipient as well. These are the people the project team provides information to, which they then digest and determine whether their funds are going to desired results.

- **End User or Target Audience**: This is the recipient (or desired recipients) of the project's value. These are the people anxiously awaiting completion and to who the project team owes an explanation of the capabilities, capacities and hidden downsides of the project. They're the owners of the warranty after the project is delivered.

- **Regulator**: This is the array of people who represent everything from licensing to taxes to safety to zoning to national standards of quality and funding schemes. These are the one who neither pay nor receive the benefit of the project but represent either the public interest, corporate interest, or professional interest.

Your Stakeholder Family, the various sponsors, bill-payers, users, regulators, etc., needs to be well understood by your team. While we'd like to think that personal influence doesn't matter, it does. Take a look at the Relationship Mapping and Influence Mapping tools in The Toolbox for ideas on how to explicitly portray the various power dynamics at play in the stakeholder arena. These will help to make explicit the connections that will increase the ability to create and contribute value throughout the lifecycle of the project.

The Readiness Two

The scene is nearly set. We've addressed what's on the project table: cost, schedule, scope and quality. We've addressed who's at the project table: the in-house family, the contractor family and the stakeholder family. What's left is to look at some remaining components to our project excellence, answering the question of whether we're making sure we have food in the pantry and are ready for any bad weather that could come our way.

Entrusting Supply

Notice the word you need to have in your mind when addressing your supply and suppliers: entrusting.

Recall SIPOC in the chapter Enabling Joy (also found in The Toolbox), Deming's picture of how all work gets done. It starts with Suppliers.

In point 4 of his famous 14 Points, he makes a very powerful statement about how to interact with your suppliers: "End the practice of awarding business on the basis of price tag. Instead, minimize total cost. Move toward a single supplier for any one item on a long-term relationship of loyalty and trust."

Your suppliers are the food for your project. Getting materials and services when the project needs them is critical to project progress and team health. Lead this effort by connecting with suppliers as trusted partners, not as suspicious dealers from the black market or the price-cutting winner of a bidding war.

Enabling this entrustment is addressed later in the IDEAL Approach. The point here is to take note that building a relationship with suppliers that ensures not just a ready and reliable supply but also expands the overall problem-solving, value-creating power of the project team requires leadership, not ledgership based on spreadsheet results alone.

Intuiting Risk

Risk.

My simple definition is this: Risk is when something *might* happen that you wish wouldn't. Risks are not a sure thing. And looking out over the horizon of your epic adventure, you can only guess at or sense risk. After all, if something is definitely going to happen, it's no longer a risk at all; it's a known condition.

I state the obvious here to point out that identifying and dealing with risk is part of the human experience, and a very interesting one at that. Think of it this way: Your project is based on a lot of predictions about how much, how soon, with whom and by when. And those predictions may or may not come true.

In many ways, setting a goal and working toward it requires a calculated leap of faith. Sure, as experienced project professionals, we put safety nets under that leap.

But it's still a leap in the end.

Now, keep in mind that risk isn't just about the possibility of something bad coming true. It's also about potentially not seeing opportunities to do something great: the risk of not capitalizing on an opportunity that could benefit your project.

To make this flip side more explicit, many organizations complement risk identification with opportunity identification. (Though the M-word is how others shabbily describe what to do.) In addition to sensing possible detriments to project success, encourage your team to always be on the lookout for possible opportunities to enhance the outcome in worthwhile ways. For example, if we can get what seems like an immovable constraint removed, what would that open the door to accomplish?

The practice of getting comfortable with this state of existence goes by many names, such as risk assessment, risk management, risk avoidance and risk analysis. With that said, those labels don't matter much. What does is how the entire process first starts with the truly human gift called intuition. It's then shared and addressed only when the team has built the connections necessary to allow trusting dialogue.

We'll talk more about dialogue later. But first, did you catch the main point of that last paragraph? Let's repeat it: The entire discipline of addressing risk, which looks so methodical, actually starts with intuition.

Intuition, dialogue and trust all involve relying on that part of the brain that's slow: the neo-cortex part. I hope you're quickly seeing that, if you want your team to address risk well, you need to enable joy to engage members' neo-cortexes to do the kind of thinking and trusting that this component of engaging excellence requires. Without the strength from joy, your team will likely use their old brain, which will then hijack good analysis and resort to seeing all risks as monsters under the bed.

Risk intuiting and identifying occurs all through a project lifecycle, but in particular in the Explore phase.

The Toolbox has several tools for helping your team make their risk intuition explicit. The first one is a set of templates, on for classic risk, and the other for opportunities. Sometimes referred to as a matrix, these templates provide a quick-hit way to prioritize risks as they're identified. These templates provide a visual graphic to compare the identified risks and opportunities. Keep in mind, that these templates only account for the likelihood and impact dimensions of risk.

The second tool, called a Risk of Failure Template, provides a way for the team to look at all three dimensions of risk: likelihood, impact and detectability. The intent for using this template is to translate subjective perceptions of the identified risk scenario into quantifiable terms to promote the team's alignment and agreement on what actions to take to address the risk. While this template is based on a common tool called Failure Mode Effect Analysis, or FMEA, it's simplified to a template that helps classify and rank: 1) the odds of something happening, 2) how much it will hurt if it does, and 3) what warning signs, if any, might show up.

While traditional FMEAs have all sorts of cool ranking and scoring methods, I recommend that you first use The Toolbox version as a conversation tool. Keep people aware of those three dimensions of risk to promote a way to think them through. Stay alert to the fact that many times risks can be reduced by increasing their detectability.

In the D and E junctures of the IDEAL Approach, you will see there are specific opportunities to mature the team's intuitions about risks and opportunities into explicit actions for the team to take. It's critical that the team make these intuitions explicit so that the team can align on the importance and urgency of the actions to take. Use the tools to drive alignment.

Nico opened his mouth, but Dayzie plowed on. "I got it wrong. I tried to manage all these changes from control and predictability perspectives; I robbed them of their joy by failing to connect them to the new way, by failing to make sure we maximized their ability to create value, and by clouding the path for them to contribute that value." Tom, who normally had a perfect poker face, showed a bit of amused surprise at Dayzie's passionate plea to understand. "I think I see the point. We probably all veer toward classic command-and-control management styles when the going gets uncertain. But this connect, create, and contribute directive makes for a pretty good way of evaluating where we, as leaders, may be sucking the energy out of our teams."

– From <u>Enabling Joy</u>

Think It Through. Make It YOURS

1. There is emphasis in the business world on these four rational build-ing blocks of project success. They're what most project dashboards, metrics, status reports, etc., cover. Could you get The Rational Four component correct and not have a successful project?

2. Does your project or organization have an incentive based on just these rational four building blocks? In other words, if you met these four by being a bully-leader, would you still get the incentive (e.g., bonus, promotion, the next juicy assignment)? If yes, then what is the incentive really incentivizing?

3. When you need incentives (i.e., extrinsic motivators), what does that really tell you about your ability to lead through enabling joy and en-gaging excellence?

4. How transparent is your interaction with your suppliers? Are you and your team developing the rapport needed for the suppliers to be part of the project team?

5. Intuiting risk is predominantly an exercise in 'what could go wrong,' 'what might ruin the project.' How will you promote good risk iden-tification, assessment and mitigation and still enable joy?

7. Risk is three dimensional – impact, likelihood and detectability. However most people obsess over the impact (severity). What is your plan to help your team focus on all three dimensions and not get distracted by the high impact risks, the proverbial monsters in the closet?

Sipping her coffee, she swallowed and tapped the page twice for emphasis. "Okay. Yes. We're not going to stop risk management or project management, I'm sure. But I think you're right that we were thinking that was all we needed to do. We tried to lead by managing instead of leading the change the managing the risk."

"Wow! That sound kind of cool" She stared at her coffee in playful amazement. "What's in this coffee you got me?"

– From <u>Enabling Joy</u>

ENGAGE EXCELLENCE

Rational 4   Relational 3   Readiness 2

Communication:
The Vital Bond

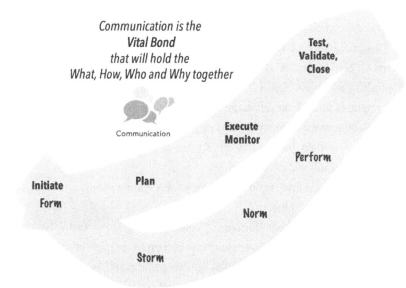

Communication is the
Vital Bond
that will hold the
What, How, Who and Why together

Test,
Validate,
Close

Communication

Execute
Monitor

Perform

Initiate
Form

Plan

Norm

Storm

Communication is **vital**. It's the life-defining bond that holds together the elements of enabling joy with the components of work excellence. With communication, joy and excellence are dynamically bonded, akin to how atoms bond, sharing electrons, to become different molecules. Communication will be the reality-defining yet change-capable connection of joy and excellence.

69

The Project Management Body of Knowledge (PMBoK) by PMI[13] suggests that 75%-90% of a project manager's time is spent on communicating. Another PMI report revealed that over 50% of the at-risk investment in a project is due to ineffective communications.[14] That same report suggests that the most crucial success factor in project management is… wait for it… effective communications to all stakeholders.

Communication is a critical core competency to all organizations. And you as a leader cannot *afford* to overlook the impact that it will have on your project if you don't take this to heart.

Sadly though, it's easy to overlook the vital necessity of this kind of informational interaction. How well a team understands its ability to communicate rarely shows up on project reports, ledgers, schedules or inspection checklists.

This brings us back to our word: VITAL. It doesn't just mean necessary. It means to give life to. A vital component is one that provides the animating principle of the living object.

Communication is the animating principle of your living project. You don't approach communication with the M-word. You approach it as a vital component that you will enable and engage. By example. By explicit design with the components of joy and excellence.

Communication drives connection, prompts creative energy, and opens the door to contributing value.

Now, you're probably thinking, "Yeah, yeah, I know that." However, you're also thinking, "But communication is a pretty big and shapeless topic. How do I get my arms around it to put into proper action?" In which case, let's simplify this to four primary purposes of project communication: learning, deciding, teaming and status. To achieve these purposes, we have four unique types of communication: dialogue, discussion, alignment and drumbeat.

---

[13] PMI, the Project Management Institute, is the world's leading association for those who consider project, program or portfolio management their profession, maintains the standard referred to as the PMBoK

[14] Based on the PMI 2013 *Pulse of the Profession*[TM] *Report*

Dialogue to Drive Learning

A dialogue is a learning conversation whose purpose is discovery. Facilitating a dialogue is like orchestrating a jam session, since the group bounces ideas off each other, searches for novel solutions, challenges long-held assumptions, and creates a compelling vision. This requires a leading and facilitating style that is adaptable yet ready to provide the structure necessary to evolve music out of what started as cacophony.

Dialogues evolve organically, not by agenda. So patience needs to be blended with energizing the conversation, taking seemingly radical ideas and revealing how they may have value. It's beneficial to have facilitators help with dialogues so that you as a leader can pour your energy into the learning.

Here's the challenge to you as a project leader. You are going to run into tough problems and you are going to need answers that are different from the ones you've had before, because, if the old answer worked, you'd not have the problem. You are also going to have events or outcomes happen that were undesired or unexpected for which you need to investigate the underlying causes. These situations require seeing the problem in a new light, to have a different understanding. In other words, your team needs to learn and to do that you need a learning conversation, a dialogue.

When you pull in a facilitator, expect them to be adept with methods that provide the structure, such as mind mapping, flow charting, picture making, nominal group technique, and even that oft-misused tool brainstorming. A causal analysis tool is in the Toolbox.

Dialogue is so essential, so critical, that it is also a distinct element in the IDEAL Approach, in the D juncture as you'll discover later. In that section, there will be tools called inquiry and advocacy. The Toolbox has some guidance on these if you want to start getting better at dialogue right now.

In the time conscious world of projects, it's tempting to jump to decisions. This seems expedient at the time but will usually come at the cost of long term effectiveness. If you want to truly engage excellence and enable joy, dialogue will be one of the best tools on you project leader toolbelt.

Discussion to Drive Decisions

For a discussion event, you're looking for a decision that everyone can and will own and be accountable to. This conversation is much like a courtroom, where the team is, in essence, the plaintiff, defendant, witness, jury and gallery all in one.

You as leader need to decide whether you're going to take an active part in it or not. If you are, then call in a facilitator who can be the judge, defense and prosecuting attorneys all in one.

The discussion process needs to center around listening with an intentional focus on learning, comparing evidence, and considering context and culture. You need to drive it to achieve a decision that's both rational and relational. Rationally, the decision needs to be satisfactory in a technical sense. Relationally, the decision needs to be one that the Relational Three can live with and have ownership of.

To do this, you'll need to rein in opinions that are expressed with great passion (i.e., loudly) and provide amplification for those that may be offered too softly. Put another way, you need to allow for a healthy balance between letting more expressive team members speak and prompting those who like to think it over at length to weigh in as well.

Keep this conversation visible with causal diagrams, role and responsibility charts, flow maps, benefit-versus-cost graphics, decision trees, and risk and opportunity analyses.

Alignment to Team

Alignment sessions, frequently labeled as teambuilding, are times when you need everyone to just get along and build trust.

Alignment definitely needs to be conducted at the early stages of the project. This component is explained in detail in the first juncture. It's the "I" part of the IDEAL approach.

When your project team has a lot of players who are accustomed to non-joyful assignments, it can be difficult. Think getting an unruly high school team coming off a losing season to renew their belief in themselves and their ability to win. It's a constant process of re-establishing common ground, re-connecting with each other and the team purpose, rebuilding trust and restoring confidence. Alignment may also be necessary at other times in the project lifecycle. For projects that last more than a few months, expect to refresh, or even reset, the alignment of the team.

One way or the other, it's your job to improve the lens through which team members see themselves and others. This is where personality-type tools or strength-type assessments can come in handy.

If you elect to have a facilitator help with these kinds of activity, then work with him or her to design and conduct group exercises (better thought of as scrimmages). Your goal should be to give your people a safe space to gain a fresh perspective of their own and others' ways of processing data and making decisions. These should be fun and purposeful experiments that reveal how various complex personal and system dynamics can play out.

The reason that alignment communication is frequently accomplished with exercise type events is that it's too easily preached without being understood. Exercises expose the stress points in team alignment allowing the team to take specific rather than generic actions. The building blocks of team alignment include: how well members know each other, how well trust is built or restored, how well they believe in the vision and how well they see their own roles and contributions to the project. Exercises provide a safe scrimmage space for team learning so as to be able to improve these building blocks of alignment.

Drumbeat to Know Status

Drumbeat communications are similar to the format of any periodic summary of events. It's the rhythm of keeping the project going while dialogue, discussion and alignment are the melody and lyrics. You need that rhythm because people crave a level of rhythm that grounds them through the course of the everchanging project.

While the melody and lyrics may seem to go all over the place, the drumbeat provides a reassuring rhythm.

Make your drumbeat unchanging, be it a daily check-in meeting, a weekly staff meeting or a monthly update with the customer. The meetings should have an unchanging agenda format, no matter what the content is. Similar to the structured familiarity found in both print and televised daily news, the format of the drumbeat doesn't change.

For example, if your daily check-in is a standup 15-minute deal, then it should always be a 15-minute standup. If your plan of the day has customer feedback and updates, what's planned for the next 24 hours and a rundown of how larger issues are being handled, all covered in 30 minutes, then every plan of the day has these on the agenda and is 30 minutes, regardless of how the day went. Maintaining the rhythm is critical

An often overlooked drumbeat is the one that should follow daily actions, commonly referred to as an After Action Review (AAR). This is a valuable way to implement a learning rhythm. The objective is to harvest learning continually with a known cadence. By restricting the recollection to only cover a specific action or small time period, like a day, makes it easier to both be thorough and efficient. The AAR format is a quick hit, with no written notes, only a candid sharing of observations and reflections on what was just done. There is an After Action Review cue card in The Toolbox.

No matter what periodicity or style you use for your drumbeat, it should have these key features:

- You need to establish some periodic, predictable pauses – whether they're daily, weekly, monthly or whatever – that serve as ways to validate that the team (be it the whole team, the leadership team, or the stakeholder team) hears and shares the news. The real purpose is to maintain the connections to people and purpose and ensure that the team is able to create value effectively and efficiently.

- The rhythm has to be maintained. The meeting time doesn't vary, the agenda format doesn't vary. Just like a newspaper has given sections on given days with only rare exceptions on special news days, your drumbeats have to emphasize a control and command of the project, no matter how hectic or chaotic the daily pace seems to be. You must maintain your asset mindset that you're leading the project. It's not leading you. A visible, unchanging rhythm that doesn't fall prey to urgent work items will provide a critical steadying and calming effect.

- The agenda template should have dedicated time windows that are unchanging. Remember: This is just the rhythm, not the melody or lyrics. So when a topic needs more dialogue, give it its own meeting.

- Develop a plan to maintain a flow of information on upcoming, current and past deliveries, along with accounts payable and accounts receivable.

- Have a time slot that people can reserve for deeper conversations about issues where causal analysis or brainstorming are needed. Some teams block out a time slot at the backend of the drumbeat that team members can reserve for a topic they want to go deeper on.

TAG NOTE:

Leading is *personal*. When you have geographic, cultural and time-zone spans, you must be the bridge. This means you need to petition to add funds to the project budget in order to provide travel so that you can be face to face with any non-local portion of the team and/or to bring small numbers of distanced team members to the same location as the bulk of the team.

Relying on telecommunication technology to replace human interaction is fraught with failure. Drumbeat communications serve as an anchoring and stabilizing function, and hence are optimally scheduled for the same day, same time, same duration, and same agenda format. However, if your team includes members in other time zones – especially time zones that are more than a workday out of sync with you – then consider these alternatives:

- If a large number of members are in another time zone, then schedule every third or fourth drumbeat to be at the drumbeat time in their time zone. This helps everyone appreciate each other by meeting them where they are, at least in time.
- If you're periodically visiting another project team site, then consider having the drumbeat occur there.

Think It Through. Make It YOURS

1. Common advice is that a given topic should not piggyback a discussion session right behind its dialogue session, and that at least a lunchtime – or better yet a workday – should separate the two.

   Why do you think this is a recommended practice?

2. Drumbeat meetings frequently become an arena for the blame game. How will you keep the agenda meeting to just being a news report and not a deep analysis of what went wrong or an exposé of wrongdoing? Think of what specific tool or trick you can use (alternatives to the idea in No. 5 above)

3. Studies have shown that amazing projects always have great leadership. (Interestingly, the inverse is not true. Surprisingly, some projects with great leadership have still been considered less than ideal.) Since great leadership and great communication go hand in hand, an ideal project must have great communication. Do you have a plan to check on your communication as much as you check on the schedule and cost of your project?

 **ENABLE JOY**  **ENGAGE EXCELLENCE**

Connect   Create   Contribute   **Communication**   Rational 4   Relational 3   Readiness 2

The IDEAL Approach

Okay. Time for you to get back in the director's chair.

Remember that we have two flows: our team dynamics (the romance movie archetype) and our work dynamics (the action movie archetype). They're the plot path into which we weave our components for enabling joy, engaging excellence and bonding all that together with communication.

The IDEAL approach is the way to lead this epic and transform your team's ideas into a delightful reality for the stakeholders. And while your epic adventure will be unique to you, the IDEAL Approach will provide a way to weave in proven best practices into your specific situations and needs.

Let's get started learning what the IDEAL Approach is all about.

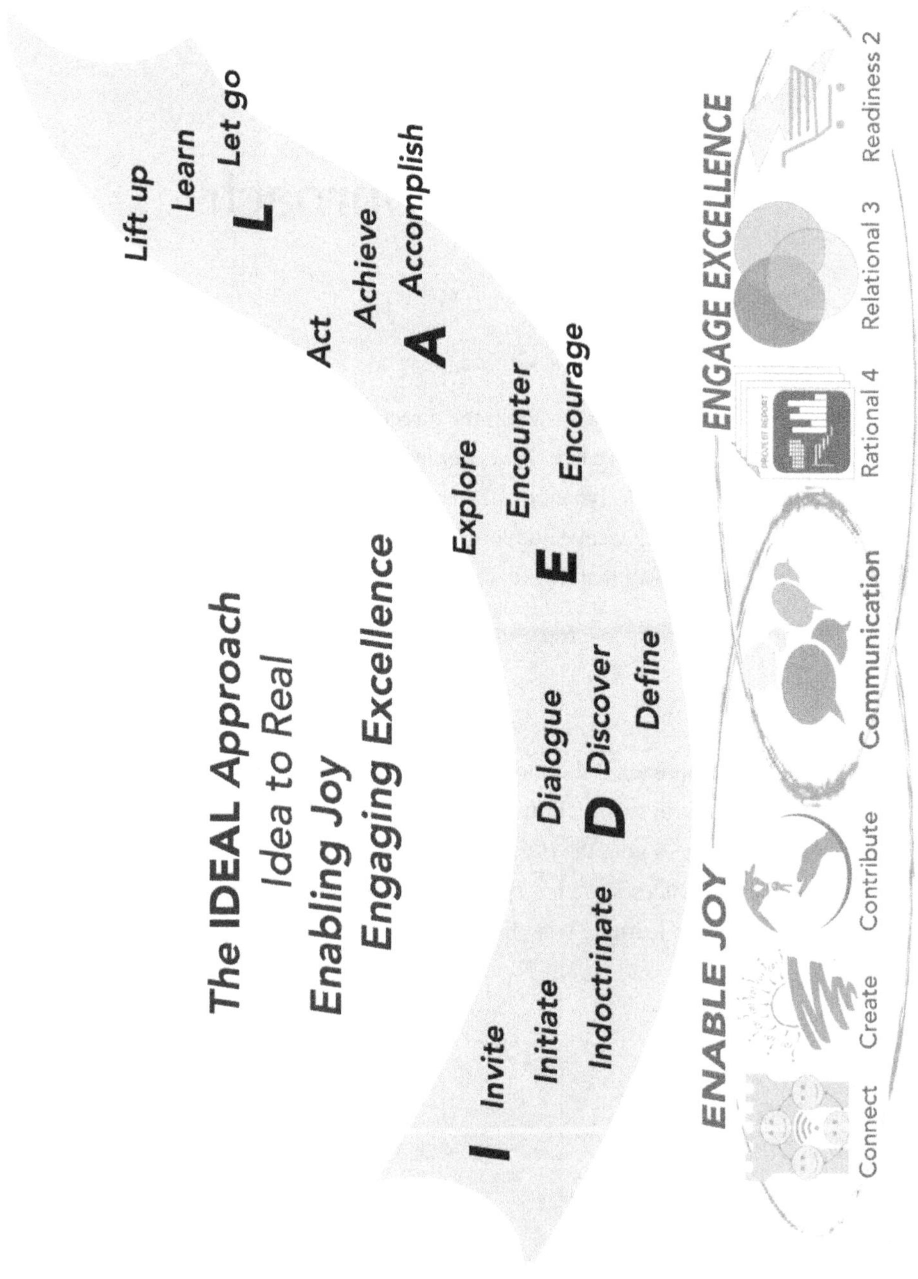

The **IDEAL** Approach
Idea to Real
Enabling Joy
Engaging Excellence

I Invite
Initiate
Indoctrinate

D Discover
Dialogue
Define

E Encounter
Explore
Encourage

A Accomplish
Achieve
Act

L Let go
Learn
Lift up

ENABLE JOY

ENGAGE EXCELLENCE

Connect Create Contribute Communication Rational 4 Relational 3 Readiness 2

Now you see why IDEAL is an acronym. Each letter of I-D-E-A-L defines what I'll call a juncture. Each juncture has three elements, each conveniently starting with the same letter. Overall, these fifteen elements are the steps you'll take to ensure that you are on an IDEAL path to project achievement and accomplishment, and beyond.

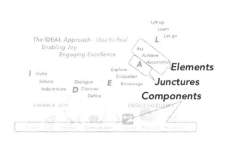

Notice that the I-D-E-A-L junctures are actually an integration of our Team Story (remember our romantic comedy?) AND our Work Story (remember our action adventure?) The three elements at each are the tangible or intentional actions you'll take to lead the IDEAL project. Many of them refer to handy tools, and those are explained in The Toolbox chapter.

The three elements that comprise each juncture reinforce and complement each other. At least one of the three primarily enables joy and at least one primarily engages excellence. The IDEAL approach continuously balances and equips you to not sacrifice team joy for project excellence and vice versa.

Notice that I refer to IDEAL as an approach. I intentionally don't call it a process or a procedure. Not even a guideline. That's for several reasons.

One, IDEAL is iterative capable. As people flex; the project matures; and budgets, scopes and constraints change, the project leader will need to continually evaluate which juncture might need to be reiterated or reinforced. For example, as new players come on the team, Invite will need to be reiterated.

Another reason it's an approach is because the elements of IDEAL are neither in lockstep nor independent of each other. There is a fluid interplay and an overall cumulative effect. Because they're balancing enabling joy and engaging excellence, they fit hand in hand versus normal process steps that fit head to tail.

Thirdly, this is for you. The IDEAL approach is a *personally* oriented project leader preparation strategy. And it's one that works, as you'll get to see firsthand once you start putting it into action.

Keep in mind that this approach integrates many proven ideas from other references and guidebooks on how to run a project. But there is a key difference: the continual and caring focus on LEADING and making it PERSONAL.

In other words, it's about **people with a purpose** interacting with an ever-changing story that **transforms an idea into a reality.** It involves so much more than just getting a job done. It's about **making a valuable difference** for both customer and team.

This is why you have to enable joy in leading the IDEAL project. That valuable difference will be real strength of this endeavor and will be the way that you as leader create and contribute leadership value to the team.

To help keep components, junctures and elements untangled, I'll use our graphics along the way. For each element, I will highlight which components of enabling joy, engaging excellence and communication are being especially enabled, engaged and expressed.

For example, for the element Initiate, I'll have this graphic below showing that the approaches and tools described in the element Initiate enable a greater ability to Connect, Create and Communicate, as well as make the most out of the Relational Three.

I've intentionally kept all the components visible because each I-D-E-A-L juncture helps in some way to enrich joy, excellence and communication.

Let's begin our IDEAL approach.

IDEAL: Invite, Initiate, Indoctrinate

The **IDEAL** *Approach*
Idea to Real
Enabling Joy
  Engaging Excellence

I Invite
  Initiate
    Indoctrinate

D Discover
  Define
  Dialogue

E Explore
  Encounter
  Encourage

A Act
  Achieve
  Accomplish

L Lift up
  Learn
  Let go

Are you ready to begin your project? And before you say yes or no, how do you know the answer to that?

Remember, you're only at the boy-meets-girl part and the action adventure threshold of your epic. The care you invest in these Invite, Initiate and Indoctrinate elements will set the stage for the roller coaster ride of project life inevitably kicks into high gear. I've never met a team that, at the conclusion of the project, said they should have spent less time preparing, team building, or creating or communicating their vision. This juncture does this.

While on the surface, this may look like the stage that's simply about getting together, learning names, discovering personalities, understanding the goal of the project and setting the timeline... it's deeper than that. This is your window to connect your team to the purpose of the project or, more personally, YOUR purpose of the project.

People need to know why YOU are invested in this.

INVITE

> **Proactive Mindset:** Lead based on what you have, not what you don't.
> You are not a victim of estimates, changes or schedule. You have choices.
>
> **An Attitude of Gratitude:** Gratitude comes first, not later. Appreciate the
> people, the project and the opportunity.

This initial stage is where everyone is just getting their head around what the project will, can and will be all about.

Having Invite as the first step reminds you to do it again whenever a new person joins a project. While the best practice is for the project team to stay together from beginning to end,[15] that is frequently not an option.

As leader, use the "invite" word when soliciting or requesting team members. It sets the stage for two powerful foundations.

The first foundation is a proactive tone. I use the word "proactive" in the sense of being able to make choices: to not be a victim. A proactive person understands that he or she *chooses* to work a certain job to support his or her lifestyle. A non-proactive person, on the other hand, *has* to go to work.

Another way to understand this is to realize it's opposite: reactive. Seeing oneself as a victim is reactive, while seeing oneself as having a choice is responsive. If you're waking up in the morning saying to yourself, "I have to do this or that," then you're painting your world in a reactive light.

As a leader, you set the proactive orientation. And by inviting team members onto the project, you reinforce that being a team member is a choice.

---

[15] Adapted from *Winning at New Products*

The other foundation you're setting here is one of gratitude. When you invite someone to an event, you're grateful they attend. While it may seem too early to be in the thankful mode, it's nonetheless critical.

Gratitude is actually supposed to precede the action that is thanked though. Being grateful is an attitude for enabling joy, especially the connect element of it. That connection is key for achieving psychological safety,[16] which is the main outcome of the initiate element.

Gratefulness and proactive orientation feed on each other. And beginning your project with explicit gratitude also builds what Shawn Achor refers to as rational optimism. It's the ability to see problems as fixable.

Achor quotes a study that optimism beats smarts by 35%. Admittedly, I really don't know how they measure that stuff. But studies have shown that the three biggest predictors of success are:

1. Optimism (a belief that our behavior matters)
2. Strong social connection
3. Perceptions of stress as a challenge (more on this in the Encourage segment).

Two undercurrents are likely that you need to counter at the get-go. Remember, there's never a second chance to make a first impression.

The first undercurrent is frequently that people feel like they've been assigned to the project. And from an organizational accountability perspective, this could be true. That's why, at the risk of being repetitive, you need to invite people to be on the team, not force, coerce or conscript them. They're not prisoners of the project.

I know that in the reality of life, it seems that a lot of folks end up on teams because there's no one else available or because we just have to have so-and-so. But there's no need for you as the leader to extrapolate on that initial reason.

---

[16] Psychological safety is the term given to the key ingredient in successful teams as found by the Google study Project Aristotle performed in 2012 and reported in various sources.

You must reinforce that we all have a choice in the attitude we bring to the project.

Your job is to connect each person so that that he or she feels invited to be on the journey.

The second undercurrent is that organizational tension that exists in many matrix organizations, where the people on the team are conflicted as to whether you're their boss or whether their organizational or department supervisor is their boss – yet another reason to think "invite" rather than "conscript" or "steal," as is the frequent sentiment held by departmental supervisors.

This invitation to the project needs to be well agreed upon between you and the person whom your team members rely on for getting paid and promoted. You need to step in and lead that agreement process.

An idea to try: At your periodic team meetings, make it a habit to ask several folks to share something they're grateful for that happened in the last 24 hours. While it would be best if they shared a gratitude to someone on the team, start simple.

You may want to focus the gratitude to something in or about the team. Saying "I'm grateful for such a great team" is too generic. It needs to be personal and specific.

The U.S. Navy Blue Angels are a team of pilots who fly highly dangerous, unforgiving formations and maneuvers for the U.S. Navy at air shows. During their post-flight briefs, they share what they could do better and end their individual statements with 'glad to be here'... a reminder that they're grateful for the honor to serve in the Blue Angels – no matter how well they performed in the show.

INITIATE

Project team members co-process their project world. Recall that strong social connections are the second-biggest predictor of success (after optimism) and the greatest predictor of long-term happiness. So you need to provide a team culture that promotes and nurtures a co-processing state of existence, which is officially known as psychological safety. That term works well because it sets what it's describing on the same kind of level as physical safety – which everyone recognizes is important.

Psychological safety is the enabler for each person to share their expertise, their perspectives and their concerns without fear of retribution or shunning. To begin this process is why many team leaders choose to have some type of team-building exercise at this early stage of the project. It may be a shared adventure like rope courses or an office party. Doesn't matter…

What's critical is that you clearly understand and communicate that the objective is to achieve psychological safety so that team members can truly CONNECT. The whole team needs to know they can share new ideas, contrary ideas, candid feedback and concerns, and without fear that they'll be ostracized, either openly or covertly.

Let's repeat that. The type of event is important, but the true goal is to increase connection – to each other and to the team's purpose.

Why is this critical? The blood cells of a team are the continual and everchanging flow of trust. That's what nourishes the team to be together. As such, keep that purpose in mind in anything you do. Never forget that you're there to initiate the building of trust every bit as much as to get the project done.

In that pursuit, being entertaining and keeping it humorous have their places as well – and very good places at that. Science supports the link between the chemicals in our brain that drive happiness and those that drive trust. So here's what you need to keep foremost in your plan: Keep the goal of engendering mutual respect in a relaxed, maybe even fun, atmosphere.

Many times, teambuilding events draw upon a narrow skillset, like building with blocks or being good at a given game. With that in mind, have several events to round out the appeal to all members of your team. Finding additional possibilities shouldn't be hard... only narrowing them down.

Essentially, teambuilding comes in all sorts of flavors and intensities. It's its own industry, complete with a swarm of consultants. Feel free to utilize them if you'd like. But as leader, make sure to own your teambuilding process and stay focused on its core purpose to implant psychological safety.

An idea to try: This idea is based on a concept in the book, *The Most Human Human*. In it, author Brian Christian talks about how the Turing test – which is meant to test the human-level reactiveness of a computer – actually teaches us what it means to be alive: to be truly human. That and, funny enough, how to make the most out of speed dating.

The official version of speed dating, as developed by Yaaco Deyo, forbade talking about what participants do for a living (i.e., the resume stuff) and where they've lived (i.e., the historical stuff). This means that speed daters have to BE their human selves, not just describe themselves.

Moreover, restricting this deep conversation to a short timeframe measured in minutes bubbles up a way to discover deeply intimate truths about ourselves and others. And transferring that same spirit to our team settings can be just as rewarding. Pairing off team members in rows of facing chairs without tables, we're able to get eye to eye.

As leader, be sure to set the ground rules and go for it, conducting each round as needed. I'd recommend engaging a facilitator so that everyone on the team is participating, including you. (The Toolbox has a template for setting this up.)

The point here is that psychological trust has to be thoughtfully built. You can't rely on casual conversation to produce the needed tight bonds between people. As we stated in our discussion on Communication, real dialogue is about learning. It's therefore uncomfortable and challenging at times.

That's why this process of Initiate needs a leader.

In this Initiate element, you need to sow the proper seeds in order to harvest learning at the conclusion of the project: what you will see during the Learn element in the L juncture of the IDEAL approach. And since you're the director of this project epic, you're allowed to take a peek at the ending – that is, the L juncture – to help you put in place the foundation to Learn later.

The conclusion of this project may very likely be the bridge to another project for many on the team, including yourself. One of the drivers of joy is learning, since learning provides new ways to connect, create, and contribute. You need to set the stage for fruitful learning. A straightforward method to capture that potential is to keep a diary, a logbook, or a running set of observations. That way, at the conclusion of the project, you have the whole picture.

This is critical. Because, at the end of the project, our minds will be full of what we struggled with in the last moments alone, not over the course of the project. Likewise, we need a way to put the whole story in context: to see how earlier twists in the plot affected decisions and outcomes later on.

There are several ways to plant this seed. But keep in mind that, like a seed, these ideas need to be watered and tended to throughout the project lifecycle.

An idea to try: Recruit a journalist. This can be done in many ways. One would be to hire an intern: someone who's taking technical writing or even journalism. Another would be to actually hire a journalist. You could also give the task to someone on the team: someone with the best vantage to be objective in observing and capturing the project story.

For an excellent example of this idea in action, read the Pulitzer Prize-winning book *The Soul of a New Machine* by Tracy Kidder. He uses it to detail how he was an embedded journalist in a computer design project team. And what he found was fascinating.

For learning to occur, the journalist needs to be able to see what the team cannot see for themselves. He or she has to capture the dynamics of joy and excellence being enabled and engaged respectively. The benefit will be that, at the end of the project, you'll have as close to an objective replay of the project epic as you can expect to reveal lessons to learn.

An idea to try: Set up a plan for retrospectives. A retrospective is exactly what it sounds like: a look back to get a perspective on what happened, why it happened, and how to learn from the experience. (There is a guide for retrospectives in The Toolbox.)

The goal of a retrospective at this Initiate point is to plant the idea that the team will have periodic pauses to reflect on how it went, with the goal of spotting any course corrections that can be made. There should also be an overall Retrospective at the end of the project to explicitly learn from this project epic.

A typical approach to retrospectives is to conduct them at least at the end of each project lifecycle phase, namely initiating, planning, executing, testing, validating and closing.

The retrospective idea works well in concert with the embedded journalist idea.

TAG NOTE:

This can be done, though not as powerfully, with video chat tools. This is a rare instance when face-to-face videos are an actually viable substitute for face-to-face interactions.

Suggest that when a local team member is paired with a remote team member, they use a personal device to video chat. They may need to step aside from the big group to reduce distraction for each other.

INDOCTRINATE

ENABLE JOY | **ENGAGE EXCELLENCE**

Connect   Create   Contribute   Communication   Rational 4   Relational 3   Readiness 2

> *Key ingredients:*
>
> **Vision Alignment** – *Sharing, believing, and being inspired and ready to aspire to a future state that is more than just the contract.*
>
> **Values Adoption** – *Personal ownership and unwavering adherence to ethics or principles that drive (and are pervasive in) all team decisions.*

Contrary to the negative understanding of the term today, to indoctrinate simply means to imbue with an idea.

Your project starts as an idea that the team will transform into a reality. And your vision is an image of that accomplishment at its best outcome. Along the way, there will be countless decisions to be made by the project team members, and you'll need to ensure that certain inviolable values are always driving those decisions.

The Indoctrinate element is your preparation period to imbue each team member with that vision and those values. Why does a project need a vision? Isn't being on time and on budget per contract sufficient?

The mission – the purpose – of the project is clear. It defines the desired output. It is to achieve an on-time, in-budget, in-scope project in a safe, ethical way. Timeliness, cost and quality are outputs of the project along with its actual content. Meanwhile, achieving the mission and delivering the outputs is the tangible and required duty of a project team.

But vision doesn't begin and end there. It speaks to the outcome.

While the objective of the project may be as grandiose as to build a gothic cathedral in the center of Paris in a 350-year timeframe, that's only the output. The outcome is a world-renowned building that speaks to the character of the nation, symbolizes the beliefs and hopes of the people, and gives the worshipping congregations a small glimpse of the castle set aside in eternity by their God. The project vision is much more than making sure the gargoyle subcontractor delivers granite ghouls for the gutters on time.

You have to provide an explicit visibility to the outcome, or its vision will get lost in the swarm of details of achieving the mission. Ideally, the vision will be that lifeline you can pull on when the team or project hits those swampy bogs that stall team dynamics and stymie progress.

Your project vision must have aspirational, not just inspirational, value. Inspiration comes from an external source. It's just the spark. Aspiration, however, is the fire, fueled by intrinsic motivation.

A vision that generates aspiration generates joy. Why? Because we aspire to be connected. We aspire to have purpose: to create value and contribute to that purpose. Vision needs to speak to the accomplishment of a desired outcome, not to the achievement of the required outputs and contract conditions.

Then there are values, which are more than just a sign in the office. Another reason we use Indoctrinate is because there are some values you want to make sure are never sacrificed during the course of the project.

For example, when an endeavor involves rigorous physical activity, one of your inviolable values needs to be looking out for each other's safety. You should indoctrinate that value from the start. When the endeavor deals with sensitive organizational information or personal health information, then you should indoctrinate a value to respect privacy and security.

Value indoctrination is a discipline that requires repeated emphasis and explicit practice. It's common practice in projects that involve dangerous machinery or electricity for safety to be a daily meeting topic. Team members are given a full run-down in this regard so that they are thoroughly informed.

As the leader, you need to discern the inviolable values and know how to reinforce them. You'll also have to work hard to hold the highest standard in keeping those values, since your team will be watching what you say and do. If they see you texting while driving into the parking lot, they'll question your adherence to the value of safety. If they hear you sharing sensitive information to outsiders, they'll question your adherence to the value of security.

Indoctrinate pulls the group together with a common vision, a common set of values. This plants the basis for alignment. This is critical. Because enabling joy does entail enabling each person's role to create value. This is empowering. But without intentionally indoctrinating your team, without imbuing them with the agreed upon mission, vision and values, that empowering nature of enabling joy could lead to what looks like anarchy. Empowerment without alignment is just what is sounds like; lots of energy and creative output going in all sorts of directions. That is not ideal.

Indoctrinate is one of the initial steps that project leaders want to skip over. They have a scope of work, a schedule and a budget and that would appear to make sufficient marching orders. It would if all you want from your team is for them to rent their time to you in exchange for mindless compliance to whatever you say. That is not ideal.

Putting in the effort to invite, initiate and indoctrinate will pay dividends that will not be apparent at first. Doing it poorly will be like a shoddy foundation that looks good until it gets stressed. Take time to lay a solid foundation.

TAG NOTE:

Values needs to resonate across geographic and cultural spans. For example, having a value that team members can always "speak up" may resonate well in the northeastern American office. But it won't resonate as well in the Mumbai or Tokyo offices.

Think It Through. Make It YOURS

1. Contractors and subcontractors are often smeared with the notion that they're "just contractors," as if that means they're less passionate about the success of the project (or less qualified or not able to understand the organization's perspective). How will you connect your contractors to the vision and core team members? And how will you help them be engaged in project success?

2. Anyone can get output from a team of A-game players. But on average, people are average. That's okay. Average can still produce excellence. How are you going to keep the team unified when some will inevitably appear to be doing more work than others?

3. How will you invite the team to co-create and/or take ownership of the vision?

4. Competitive-style teambuilding events have the benefit of cranking up the engagement. However, you're building a team that needs to develop their ability to cooperate. How can you blend the beneficial intensity of competition with the need to build cooperation?

5. What expectations of the customer, stakeholders, regulators or financiers will it be difficult for your project team to believe they can create value toward (i.e., which expectations seem unachievable)? How will you bridge that gap?

6. What outcomes (in addition to tangible outputs) are you envisioning this project will accomplish for the end users and/or customers?

7. What outcomes will being on this project team accomplish for the team members themselves?

8. What Outcomes could this project accomplish for contractors and subcontractors?

9. What are some current realities on your project or team that will probably come out during the invite, initiate or indoctrination efforts that may have a negative influence on psychological safety? Jot down your thoughts on how you'll need to go about leading and facilitating the Invite, Initiate and Indoctrinate elements to build on the positive influences for psychological safety.

   (E.g., *team building events that don't lead to competition, participative workshops where the team shares what attributes will be the fruit of the project team values and how they will know whether values are being lived up to, etc.*)

10. What values for your project must be so well indoctrinated that they become unquestioned and unwavering? Be specific as to why.

11. People want to run toward a vision. Many project teams default to a vision of on-time and on-budget. Does your project vision compel aspiration to an IDEAL project? Jot down ideas that would make your vision more compelling than on time, on schedule, in scope.

One of the most popular rock stars of the last four decades has been Bruce Springsteen, popularly known as The Boss.

Interviews with his longtime drummer, Max Weinberg, have shed light on how tight of a team the Bruce's E-Street Band really was. Apparently, at any given concert with 25 songs, maybe 12 of those songs could be different from what he wrote down an hour before. Max talked about how he and the band members really needed to keep their eyes and ears on him, but that it felt normal.

After years of playing together, when the Boss went in one direction, the rest of the band got pretty good at just going with him. It's also interesting that this was true because The Boss wasn't just giving the concert he planned: He was giving the concert the audience wanted. He'd developed a feel for the audience or would respond accordingly when someone held up a sign.

What does this say to you about how The Boss defined delivering each concert "project"? Was it more than just on-time, on-budget? Were these concerts performance-to-plan or amazing performances? And could he have achieved the vision he had for the concert without the completely engaged alignment and formation of his team?

IDEAL: Dialogue, Discover, Define

The **IDEAL** Approach
Idea to Real
Enabling Joy
Engaging Excellence

Lift up
Learn
Let go
L

Act
Achieve
Accomplish
A

Explore
Encounter
Encourage
E

I Invite
Initiate
Indoctrinate

Dialogue
D Discover
Define

So there you are, with the project looking like it's off to a great start. You've invited each player in turn, initiated their bonding as a team and indoctrinated them into vision and values. Their heads were nodding up and down, and smiles were on the faces.

However, team members – and you as their leader – are finding out that maybe they don't have the same expectations, agenda and motivation they all thought they did. Everyone's starting to wonder what they got themselves into.

Welcome to the part where the villain is starting to look unbeatable, and/or there's a spat between our boy and girl.

There's a well-founded reason for anxiety to be setting in right about now. Mihaly Csikszentmihalyi – a Hungarian-American psychologist who published multiple studies on happiness and creativity – recognized and named a psychological concept called Flow. This concept has a cool explanation of how people feel "in the flow" when the work and their skills are well-matched. (i.e., when they're confident and content in how they can and will create value.)

Therefore, Flow is an indicator in work when joy has been enabled.

Anxiety and worry are indicators that our perceptions of our skill level are low: that we won't be able to create or contribute or otherwise experience joy in the project. (Remember that the opposite of joy is fear; and anxiety and worry are its bitter fruits.)

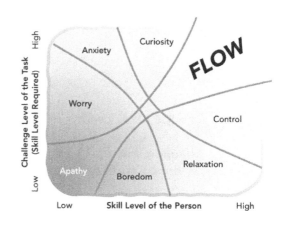

Seeing the challenge of our project in that negative light isn't uncommon at this stage. You need to be prepared for this dip into the valley of despair, where the bonds the team just started building are already being strained.

How so? It's a process of intentional learning followed by enlightened decision making. This is where dialogue and discussion that we defined earlier will be critical.

This is where you need to force into view those daunting realities that make this project a true challenge. You must first lead learning – that's Dialogue and Discover. You then can best lead making those initial decisions – that's Define. While we have these three D components, the world seems to only see Define, with its tangible schedules, work lists and budgets.

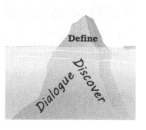

As the leader, you must make Dialogue and Discover just as intentional, since they ensure the effectiveness of Define. They're like the much larger underwater part of an iceberg that enables the visible portion above the surface.

DIALOGUE

ENABLE JOY ———————— **ENGAGE EXCELLENCE**

Connect Create Contribute Communication Rational 4 Relational 3 Readiness 2

> *Key ingredients:*
>
> **Advocacy:** *Helping others to see and challenge our assumptions around the facts so as to strengthen or revise them.*
>
> **Inquiry:** *Helping others to help us understand their assumptions around the facts so that we may better compare them to our own assumptions.*

As explained before, the purpose of Dialogue is to learn. It opens up options, ideas, tangents and alternatives. It is NOT the decision-making conversation though. That's Discussion.

The team is looking to you to be decisive regardless. Everyone wants to know what is coming up next, what to expect and what to do. And, admittedly, that tends to tilt your bias toward having discussions. But short-circuiting the learning process is neither efficient nor effective in the long term.

Dialogue is the opportunity to find the best answers, to consider the what-if scenarios, to seek alternative paths, and to entertain ways to delight and not just satisfy the customer. Dialogue begins here, encouraging skills that will be needed again in the elements of Explore and Encounter.

Dialogue is laying out all the assumptions, risks and unknowns. It's team learning and team training meant to expand the members' collective mind about how to go about this project in ways that will eliminate problems they've seen before and give credibility to new tasks.

Recall that a team co-processes the realities and experience of the project. Dialogue makes that co-processing visible.

Keep in mind that it's only effective if you've adequately stepped through the Invite, Initiate and Indoctrinate elements already. That's because putting an assumption on the table is risky, and each person needs to have the psychological safety to know their assumption will be respected regardless of its final acceptance.

After all, alignment with the vision is necessary to distinguish purely crazy ideas from seemingly crazy but actually innovative ideas. And sometimes, you need to say it out loud and discuss it in order to weed out one from the other. Adoption of values needs to be proven in this planning stage first before the hectic pace of executing the project.

Dialogue also provides a way to creatively build your business case if that's required. Frequently, projects in this early stage still aren't fully funded and are therefore competing for organizational priority and resources. So Dialogue is an effective approach to fully address the projects return on investment.

Skillful Dialogue relies on two interdependent conversational roles: inquiry and advocacy. *These roles exercise the assumptions that the team members have about the facts.*

Remember: Facts are facts. So there's no real conversation about facts, but rather around what those facts mean, how they came to be, and how they affect us. That's why you need to know the following two terms:

Inquiry: Listening to learn. The skill of helping others make their assumptions around visible facts so that they can compare and contrast them to their own assumptions around the facts.

Advocacy: Making your own assumptions visible so as to invite them to be tested, explored and challenged.

The Toolbox provides templates for improving your inquiry and advocacy and how to apply those skills when the team seems at an impasse.

DISCOVER

> *Key ingredients:*
>
> **Team Learning**: *Making time to revise your limiting assumptions to see new solutions, capabilities and hidden strengths*

Discover is the natural fruit of Dialogue. Without Dialogue, there is no fruit of learning.

Not surprisingly but sadly, I've found that many teams have the Dialogue down. They even produce its fruit. But then they leave it on the tree. Just like getting actual fruit from tree to table requires an explicit harvesting, packaging and serving process, enjoying the results of positive dialogue involves a bit more than just having the conversation itself.

To harvest learning, you need to explicitly answer these two questions:

- What do we know now that we didn't when we started this conversation (meeting)?

- How will this new knowledge (learning, understanding, awareness) help us better achieve a project output or accomplish a desired outcome?

To answer these in the context of improving the team's ability to enable joy and engage excellence, use these reminders as a template:

- What did this dialogue reveal about our team? Do we better understand how we absorb and analyze data, how we make things happen, how we influence stakeholders, and how we build relationships?

- What did this dialogue reveal about delighting our customer? Do we better see ways to provide products or services that may have been overlooked at initial meetings?

It's valuable for you, the team leader, to see each Dialogue and Discover process as a way to both arrive at valuable answers and to use them to discover the previously hidden strengths, skills and latent talents of team. This provides a rich picture of the team's capacity to succeed at the project, not to mention a qualitative way to move everyone to the area of enabled joy, or, as we described earlier, being in the flow.

Dialogue and Discover both provide such rich insights on whether your team is well-matched with respect to task-related skills. This will also provide a forum to resolve concerns regarding the team's ability to connect, create and contribute.

DEFINE

ENABLE JOY --- ENGAGE EXCELLENCE

Connect Create Contribute **Communication** Rational 4 Relational 3 Readiness 2

> *Key ingredients:*
>
> **CLEAR goals** – *Ensuring that our goals keep joy and excellence in sync.*
>
> **Outputs schedules, charts, agendas** – *The common tools that serve us in enabling our team to stay connected, create value and contribute.*
>
> **Drumbeat (rhythm)** – *The steadying rhythm that provides a necessary familiarity through every changing project.*

This is the opportunity for the team to establish goals and points of common reference that provide definition for what to connect to, as well as to figure out what needs to be created and for what it will be contributing.

To maintain the connection between people and project needs, this Define element is when you'll lay out your goals. To best enable joy and engage excellence, you need to make your goals **CLEAR**.

<u>C</u>ollaborative – Is the goal structured to invite the varied talents and strengths of the team? Is it expressed and measured in a way that encourages working together?

<u>L</u>imited – Is each goal packaged to make it easy to talk about and comprehend? Loosely or broadly stated goals are difficult to connect with and create value toward.

<u>E</u>motional – Is each goal something people care about? What about appealing? The term "emotional" seems like something we'd want to exclude from our goals. But goals are fueled by inspiration *and* aspiration, two elements that are more emotional than intellectual.

Appreciable – Is each goal packaged so that it can be clearly communicated, complete with connections to that successive goals? Can it be given a clearly definable ownership, as in who's in charge of making it happen?

Refinable – Is each goal resilient enough to accommodate the reality that all plans are temporal (i.e., they're only valid based on the information and reality at the time they were created)? Refinable goals flex to accommodate the ever-changing realities of project life.

In this Define element, you'll deploy your typical tools that set the timing, flow and delivery of project outputs: the schedules, Gantt charts, S-curves or whatever work-scheduling, load-balancing tools your organization uses. You can use CLEAR as a guide for defining goals, milestones, and even key events that are part of the project work plan.

These tools are an art and discipline of their own accord. We won't cover those in this book, but let's emphasize what the real value is of those scheduling tools anyway.

Those _tools are put in place to serve us, not for us to serve them._ They tell your team where to be and when, what to do, and who all is involved. Their value is only as good as they help your team to connect to tasks, define what work items they'll create and – by seeing the downstream flow of work items – know how specific work items will contribute to accomplishing the project.

Note the language here. Traditionally, the schedule would be described as telling us when we have to work on such and such and when it's due. As an enabling joy leader though, this language won't serve you well if you want to continue what you started in the Invite element, where you planted the proactive orientation that you and your team are in control, and that you're leading this project – it's not leading you.

You want to re-emphasize that you and your team aren't prisoners or servants of the schedule. The schedule serves you.

As such, Define is when you set the rhythm for the next juncture of Act, Achieve and Accomplish. It is now you'll determine the project drumbeat, the underlying rhythm that will hold the parts of this project drama together. Recall the Status Communication – Drumbeat. Like the rhythm of a song, drumbeat sets a cadence. It's predictable and restores a sense of familiarity (i.e., connectedness) for team members when project life becomes a roller coaster.

Drumbeats provide the team with a connective rhythm, no matter how much urgent chaos is pressing on the team. And speaking of such, in the next juncture of Act, Achieve, and Accomplish, we'll take a closer look at what "urgent" really means.

Define is also a good place to begin to establish who is accountable and who is responsible for what parts of the project. Granted, ultimately, you the leader are accountable, much like the Captain of the ship when it goes aground. To help with this, take a look at the RACI tool in The Toolbox.

Sidenote: Many of you may be familiar a goal-setting process called SMART, which stands for Specific, Measurable, Attainable, Realistic and Timely. SMART goals can work very well in an operational environment but are not as valuable in the ever-changing project environment. In addition, the SMART system only suits the rational aspects of an endeavor. This would be great if we had a team of automatons: people who have no emotions. Admittedly, I have met some fairly emotionless people here and there. But they're overall rare. So plan on your team showing off the full range.

Think It Through. Make It YOURS

1. What are the current realities you see in your project that make accomplishing it seem like a super-human feat? How will you summon your team's superpowers? Do they even know they have any?

2. There's a prevailing belief that what gets measured gets done. While respecting the need to keep people connected to project status, is this statement really true? Will respect for each other on the team only get done if it's measured? What are the dangerous dark sides of your project's proposed measurements?

3. How can you structure your drumbeat meetings so that they're about more than just poking people for being late, over-budget or producing lousy outputs?

4. What has the customer or user talked about that is not part of the official scope of work or contract? Are these possible Outcomes rather than Outputs that your team should be aiming to accomplish?

5. Have your suppliers seen a complete schedule or plan for the project? Do they have a big picture view?

IDEAL: Explore, Encounter, Encourage

The **IDEAL** Approach
Idea to Real
Enabling Joy
Engaging Excellence

Lift up
Learn
L Let go

Act
Achieve
A Accomplish

Explore
I Invite
Initiate   Dialogue   **Encounter**
Indoctrinate   **D** Discover   **E** Encourage
Define

Are you ready yet? Are we getting a grip on how to beat the villain? To get the girl and guy back together?

Explore, Encounter and Encourage make up the critical juncture between planning and doing. They're the time when you'll purposely shake things up and, conversely, when you restore hope and confidence. While it seems like you can jump right from a plan to a wrench in hand, trust me when I say that would be a dangerous move.

Imagine that you and your friend have gone to an unfamiliar lake on a hot day. Once waterside in your swimsuits, you could of course just jump right in. But that would be silly. You want to first make sure that you have a way back out, that there are no warning signs posted, and so forth. *That's Explore.*

You might then lean over and dip a toe in to check depth, temperature and murkiness. *That's Encounter.* And if one of you decides not to go for it after all, the other can address those concerns and can find worthwhile reasons (not a double dare) to keep going. *That's Encourage.*

These elements – Explore, Encounter and Encourage – must happen iteratively. They're when you prompt the questions of "what if" and "how so." They're when you conduct small scale beta testing of ideas, or piloting. They're when you take proposals to the customer for their feedback.

Keeping this juncture as a set of three will interlock enabling joy with engaging excellence.

EXPLORE

Key ingredients:

Risk Awareness and Attenuation – Intuiting risk, understanding their components, agreeing on how to accept or reduce.

Opportunity Identification and Capture - Intuiting opportunities, understanding their components, agreeing on how to capture and capitalize.

Supplier Confidence – Strengthening suppliers' connection to your team.

Explore. Explore what? Explore those hidden traps. The buried treasure chests. Those concealed bridges.

This is the element that builds on the components of the Readiness Two: Intuiting Risk and Entrusting Supply. As a reminder, the tough part about exploring risk is that it's more art than science. It relies on intuition and skillful dialogue, even though the tools might make the process look like it's very methodical.

As leader, you need to help your team keep that neo-cortex engaged. This is hard because risks that have big impacts trigger the emotional responses of fight, flight or freeze, clouding our brain's attention on the likelihood dimension.

I call this the monster-under-the-bed effect. Little children waking up at night can hear a creaky noise and immediately think it's a monster, not grandma sneaking in with home-baked cookies – even though grandma would be a much higher likelihood. As leaders, you must maintain the dialogue on at least both impact and likelihood.

You might also want to seriously consider including the "can we see it coming" portion, or detectability. For instance, if there's a pretty good chance that someone would see the monster lumbering up the stairs while the family eats dinner, then that diminishes the impact. Adding this dimension allows the team to have control over risk by adding in an early warning.

The desired outcome to this Explore element is to maintain the team's pro-active orientation where they can either "create" a way to forewarn risks, buffer the impact, or reduce the likelihood. These are empowering strategies that keep the team on the path of creating value.

Explore is about not just finding sources of supplies for the project. It's to build bridges to suppliers to make them part of your team. Your challenge is to build a trusting relationship with those key suppliers that enhances their connectivity to the project and their ability to apply their expertise to maximize their value creation.

For the same reasons you may have conducted team building exercises in the Initiate phase, your team and project are well-served by inviting suppliers to a general meeting of expectations and project needs. If you evaluate them on cost alone, recognize that you're not creating team members; you're just buying the products or services based on nothing more than the price tag. That might be acceptable at times, but for critical components or schedule-critical deliveries, you need to treat suppliers as team members.

Trusting relationships will provide the creative answers to sticky project dilemmas in ways that cheap services won't.

ENCOUNTER

Key ingredients:

PDSA – *Making specific and intentional steps to experiment and learn with the Do and Study steps*

Prototypes, Betas, Pilots – *Tangible tools for Do and Study*

Journaling – *A technique to receive thoughtful input from stakeholder to enhance the Study part of PDSA.*

Encounter is the element where you'll use the proactive orientation you set during the Invite stage and put it to its greatest test: how to encounter those early indicators that this endeavor is fraught with impossible-to-beat challenges. This is when you as leader need to capitalize on these down moments and lead them into learning opportunities. To recall our movie metaphor, you are now facing the crucible moments.

As the father of nuclear power, Hyman Rickover, stated, "Success teaches nothing; only failure teaches." And C.S. Lewis, whose autobiography is titled *Surprised by Joy*, wrote, *"Failures, repeated failures, are finger posts on the road to achievement. One fails forward toward success."*

Those are truly great quotes. But this failing forward is not a natural act. Getting depressed and feeling stupid is much more common. Perhaps that's because of the attitudes we too often foster, even when we don't mean to.

When you don't enable joy, you won't enable the courage, focus, openness and respect that will enable team members to use the setbacks and surprises as learning opportunities. Nor will you have the connectedness needed for commitment to improving.[17] Instead, failures will be seen as mistakes, and that will

---

[17] Adapted from the five core values of Scrum, it's an especially agile approach to software projects.

likely degenerate into the age-old blame game.

That's why you'll need to actively steer your team into failing "forward toward success." W. Edwards Deming provides a framework to help you in this task. It's a process for learning called Plan-Do-Study-Act,[18] which is basically shorthand for the scientific method we all learned in grade school:

Plan – Put forth your idea on what might work.

Do – Try it out on a small scale, a beta test, or a rapid prototype.

Study – Determine whether it went as planned.

Act – If it did go as planned, then implement it. If not, then Plan again.

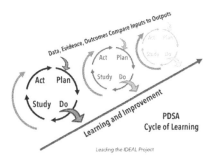

PDSA
Cycle of Learning

Leading the IDEAL Project

Of course, at this point in the project, Plan is already underway. It is what's been accomplished with the Define and Explore elements. It's likely that your team is already finding many places where the schedules, agendas, specifications, and budgets that were mapped out aren't matching the territory you're now in.

Meanwhile, Encounter involves the "Do" and "Study" steps. (Once again, the Toolbox has a complete description of the PDSA learning cycle.)

An idea to try: The U.S. Army developed a powerful yet efficient way to conduct the Study part of PDSA called After Action Reviews (AAR). The Army recognized that the natural tendency for teams on tight schedules is to react to each occurrence, short-circuiting the learning steps of Do and Study. Teams who short-circuit or cut corners on learning end up playing Whac-a-

---

[18] Originally Plan-Do-Check-Act, Check was changed to Study to better communicate the intent to Americans.

Mole,[19] whacking each setback or surprise event one at a time. And no real study occurs under those conditions.

After Action Reviews (of which there's a template for in The Toolbox) provide a way to learn, not react, by intentionally setting a time to look back on each evolution: ones that are measured in hours or maybe a few days. That way, it's easy to recall all the facts, and each person gets to speak frankly about:

- Here's what I thought we intended to do.
- Here's what I expected.
- Here's what happened.
- Here's what I saw that I didn't expect.

Another goal to explicitly Encounter with the customer and stakeholders. You're at a point where you're moving from ideas on paper to real stuff. So while your team is thinking, "Hey, we've got this all planned out!" the cost of misunderstanding customer expectations or stakeholders' requirements could actually take a quantum leap.

As team leader, you need to prepare yourself and your team to encounter those hard truths that the plan might not be perfect. And you need to solicit candid and thoughtful perspectives from customers and stakeholders on that plan. While painful as these late discoveries can be, they're necessary moments of correction to Connection that will enable a more efficient and effective stage of creating value with the Act, Achieve and Accomplish elements.

---

[19] Whac-A-Mole is a popular arcade game consisting of a waist-level cabinet with five holes in its top and a large, soft mallet. Each hole contains a toy mole. Once the game starts, moles randomly pop up for the player to whack with the mallet. The more moles whacked, the higher the player's score.

> **TAG NOTE:**
>
> Retrospectives and AARs need to include considerations for any geographic or cultural spans. That said, for both, it's nearly always better to perform these sooner than later. When retrospectives are tied to key events or milestones on a project schedule, it may be possible to schedule the retrospective early enough to support making travel plans for remote members.

An idea to try: A clever approach to removing the project team's bias is to have customers participate in what's called Think Aloud Testing. This provides a way to benefit from customer reflection on the project ideas in a way that removes the propensity for defensiveness on the part of the project team. See The Toolbox for more details.

Encounter helps you lead your team to create value even from the bitter fruit of failure, thus engaging excellence (i.e., continually improving your ability to delight the customer) and enabling joy (i.e., helping the team see better ways to connect, create and contribute). While team members and you must maintain accountability for your decisions and actions, the main goal in Encounter is not about judging what's right or wrong. It's vital that you as leader reinforce that this is about learning.

Encounter is not an easy step. It may reveal that the project and team may need to change scope, schedules, plans. This will put additional stress on your team. That is why Encounter is piggybacked with the next element, Encourage.

ENCOURAGE

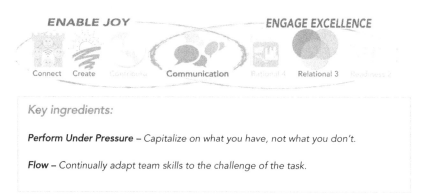

ENABLE JOY — ENGAGE EXCELLENCE

Connect   Create   Contribute   Communication   Rational 4   Relational 3   Readiness 2

Key ingredients:

Perform Under Pressure – *Capitalize on what you have, not what you don't.*

Flow – *Continually adapt team skills to the challenge of the task.*

You started team building in Initiate. Notice what I said: "started." A very necessary start, but as the project faces its crucible moments, strains will be put on the bonds that hold that team together, and that strain can make the bonds stronger or break them. Encourage is when we translate strain to strength, because, remember, joy is strength.

It's easy in the heat of battle to just bear with what you've got and go home complaining about how many headaches your team is giving you, pretending that you're the lonely hero. It's also easy to think you're being a cheerleader when you're really adding to already existent frustration levels. This happens when you say nothing more than the equivalent of "Throw a strike." or "You can do it."

Remember: By definition, projects are about changing and converting ideas to something real. That's why project teams need leaders. It's because leaders lead change. The M-word is about consistency. And while that has its place in the organizing, tabulating and scheduling aspects of project work, it's not what is needed to Encourage.

The inevitable change endemic – moving from idea to real – of the project drama puts at risk the very connections we've built. It's continually altering each team member's ability to create and contribute value. This can easily lead to frustration, which should be a signal to you that there's a lack of joy at work.

Recall the Flow model. What happens in projects is that the demands of the task change, and therefore team members feel they now have a different match of their skill level to the need. When it's an issue of tasks being less demanding than the talents of the team, that's frustration due to boredom. It's that feeling that they're wasting their energy and probably killing their career all at the same time.

In those cases, you need to think about task enrichment: giving folks more flexibility or autonomy, or the challenge to improve the way the task is done. Either way, you're looking for approaches to maximize their ability to create value, and, along the way, knock out boredom.

The other issue is more challenging. It comes about when demands are higher than the skill level, creating a growing backlog of work. As a result, anxiety sets in, leaving people feeling like they need to perform under pressure.

This is the time to encourage them, a word that has "courage" built right into it... which, in turn, is derived from the word "heart." Therefore, if you find yourself faced with an overly challenging situation, it's time to do some heart work.

This is when you might need to revisit Flow in the D juncture. You may want to refresh your understanding of how enabling joy is tied to meaningfulness as explained in the chapter on Why Joy.

We'll do that by addressing that old brain we talked about back in the beginning of the book when we were still explaining "why joy?"

Here's how it works:

1. **Engage your better self.** When anxiety creeps or even rushes in, it's necessary to take a pause. Physiologically allows people to counteract the limbic system's push toward fight, flight or freeze, keeping one's option open to use our deep-thinking brain instead. Ideas and options will only be developed by that deep-thinking brain.

2. **Relieve the pressure by reestablishing what really matters.** What do you really believe? While at that moment, the frustrations may make it look like the project is heading off the cliff, stand back and

decide what really matters. Is this current crisis really the defining moment you're making it out to be?

3. **Unhijack your neocortex.** That emotional brain is trying to save energy by telling the rational brain to stand aside. It's literally sending chemicals to shut it down, or hijack it. However, if you forcefully encourage your team to use asset thinking and simulate what IS possible when all seems hopeless… this will counteract that coup. It's simple: something along the lines of, "I can't be nice all the time, but I am able to be nice for the next 10 minutes – what would happen if I was nice for 10 minutes?" Simulate the possible.

4. **Strap on your training.** Just because panic is setting in doesn't mean your team doesn't still have all of its strengths. Get them back to what they're good at.

5. **Step out.** There's a story about training Marines to jump out of airplanes. Those who aren't fond of the idea are told to yell "Marine Corps" and just step out. It's because it reinforces a vital connection they've been indoctrinated to respect and feel protected by: a reminder that they're not going to fall alone and that it is for a worthwhile purpose besides.

6. **Excite possibility.** In the face of seeming adversity, think about what greatness would look like. Remember that you're in an action movie. So what would the daring rescue look like? By showing a point beyond the barrier staring us in the face, we can see a way to increase positive body chemistry.

7. **Reframe.** The project isn't a test. It's a challenge to live up to our standards. It's not controlling us; we're leading it.

Here's a silly but catchy way to put this guide to confident performance under pressure on a nearby sticky note.

Engage your better self – A Pause matters.
Relieve the pressure – Believe what matters.
Unhijack your neocortex – Simulate the possible.
Strap on your training – Rely on what you can do.
Step out – Marine Corps!
Excite possibility – Think greatness, not failure.
Reframe – It's a challenge to live up to, not a test.
PERFORM!

See it? Perform under Pressure? (Look at the first letters, bottom to top.)

Keep it personal.

Remind yourself that joy is strength. Encourage is when you strengthen your team.

"Good Luck. God Bless You. I'll see you in the assembly area."

- Captain Winters' remarks to his men just prior to boarding the plane to parachute into Nazi-occupied France for the D-Day invasion.

(From the HBO series, Band of Brothers)

Think It Through. Make It YOURS

1. Take a look at your work breakdown structure. Can you identify places where unCLEAR goals may hamper a team member's ability to see how he or she can create and contribute?

2. When plans inevitably change, this puts the connection to purpose at risk that was agreed upon at the start. What is your plan to periodically reconnect your team to the project purpose? To reconnect the stakeholders? To reconnect the customers?

3. Many stakeholders conduct what looks like drive-bys. They swoop in and make comments about something not being per code, per spec or per contract. That leaves a bad taste for the project team, and they soon start maligning stakeholders (hopefully not within earshot).

   How will you build and maintain respect for them anyway?

4. How will your team learn about risks? What is your plan for having an atmosphere that has great unity yet the trust to bring up black swan possibilities that could derail the project?

IDEAL: Act, Achieve, Accomplish

We're now moving from the talking to the doing: the actual conversion of specifications and lines on paper into reality. It's the messy nitty-gritty when our plans are tested by the harsh unforgiving laws of mother nature, the whims of peoples' expectations, and the perilous uncertainty of our predictions and estimates.

This is the phase where, using our movie analogy, we meet the villain hand to hand, face to face, and sneer to sneer. Therefore, this is the phase that needs to rely on resilience over the preciseness or accuracy of our plans, and where the toughness of our team's connection to purpose, adaptability to create and perseverance to contribute really comes into play.

Ideally, we're hitting our stride here. After coming through the quite likely tumultuous D and E stages (or, in drama terms, the crucible moments), we're ready to act, to accomplish and to achieve the transformation from ideas on paper to reality.

Don't be faked out though. Just like in archetypical movies, the seeming resolution of differences will frequently show that there's still a bump or two up ahead. There will likely need to be several revisits to initiating, indoctrinating, dialoguing, defining, exploring, encountering and, most definitely, encouraging. The good news is that, having done all of them before, you'll be well equipped to efficiently and effectively conduct refresh sessions of those elements.

In other words, being ready to lead the Act, Accomplish and Achieve elements will rely on how effectively you've enabled joy in Initiate, Indoctrinate, Discover, and Encourage – and how deeply you've engaged excellence in Invite, Dialogue, Define, Explore, Encounter.

ACT

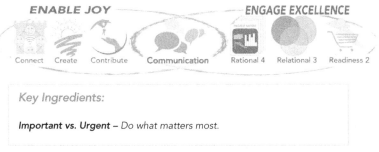

Key Ingredients:

Important vs. Urgent – *Do what matters most.*

We all know this is the time to act in a tangible, schedule-driven, time-is-of-the-essence, let's-get-'er-done way. And that's why you need to have a good priority for what you, as the team leader, act on.

You're in the tense, climatic scene of your action movie, where surprises happen regularly. The laws of Mother Nature seem to be stacked against your team's efforts, and you're wondering where the 24 hours in the day keep going.

In the midst of all that, you are the leader. You need to help your team draw strength from what they did in the I, D and E junctures. Those laid the foundation to enable joy and engage excellence for this actual transformation of idea into reality.

Struggles to fit everything into your team's schedule is inevitable at this phase. Tensions will rise. Stress will be inevitable.

As the leader, you need to pay particular attention to where you put your attention. This is the most vulnerable time to get caught up in the hectic pace and confuse something labeled "urgent" as "important." As Dwight Eisenhower, 34th president of the United States once said, "What is important is seldom urgent. And what is urgent is seldom important."

When he was the Allied commander, Eisenhower was known for his ability to put his time to good use. When asked, he shared the above quote. But he also had a tool. It's called the Eisenhower Box (or matrix).[20] (How to use the Eisenhower Box is described in detail in The Toolbox.)

As a project team leader, you're going to be assaulted with urgent tasks, requests, meetings, and the like. Every time your phone rings, it will look urgent. Your bosses, your customers, your stakeholder and your team will all want your answers, input, ideas and statuses. NOW!

In the fast and furious reality of this part of the project lifecycle, keep yourself sane and grounded. Stick to:

- Your communication plan from Define.
- Your real role: Project team LEADER.
- Your ethic: Say yes to what you can and no to the rest.
- Not using the excuses: "I'm busy" or "I was busy."

You won't improve anything using the horse's rationale in George Orwell's *Animal Farm*: "I must work harder." So don't bother saying it to yourself.

Your decisions on how to use the hours in each day will reflect your priorities to the team. So you have to consider importance first and then urgency – not the other way around.

---

[20] It was later made popular in the book *The Seven Habits of Highly Effective People* by Stephen Covey, so it's sometimes referred to as the Covey matrix as well.

A cool benefit of explicitly using the Eisenhower Box – shown here – is that it provides a picture to explain (perhaps at your periodic drumbeat meetings) what you need people to do, what you will do, and what things won't get done by anyone. Making your prioritization process visible provides a transparency of leadership that maintains their trust in your decisions.

	URGENT	NOT URGENT
	Quad I	Quad II
IMPORTANT	DO Do It Now *e.g. See Customer about Issue; Drumbeat*	DECIDE Schedule when to do it *e.g. Conduct Morale Booster; Write Reference for Intern*
	Quad III	Quad IV
NOT IMPORTANT	DELEGATE Who can do it for you *e.g. Go thru emails*	DELETE Eliminate it *e.g. Sign off Trip Reports*

The Eisenhower Box also serves as a way to help you lead the project rather than the project leading you. It will show clearly that, when you have an inkling that your team could use a four-hour realignment or team-building session, you'll be able to see it as important and not urgent... and then schedule it to replace some urgent but not important items that are clogging up the calendar.

In addition to the urgent versus important comparison, sometimes you need to sort out from a long list of options that all seem to matter in some way. For situations where the team has several efforts – maybe even sub-tier projects – to work on and can't decide which one to do first, a tool like the PICK chart may help. It's actually just a return-on-investment graph, but it's pre-loaded with a way to easily see which options should be pounced on and the ones that may look cool but really just need to be tossed aside. (Check out the PICK chart in The Toolbox.)

When results or events occur or reoccur that aren't part of the plan, and there's a likelihood of undesirable outcomes, you'll need to conduct some sort of causal analysis. These should be triggered by *any* unexpected result, not just bad ones. Causal analysis is about learning, not finding blame. It's learning by peeling back the causal factors that led to the result.

Causal analysis is a science unto itself. But here's a powerful hint: The result was caused by what DID happen, not what didn't.

When learning from an unexpected result, there's a tendency to think it happened because we didn't do such and such. For example, I got hit by a car because I didn't look both ways before crossing the street. But no. You got hit by the car because you stepped into traffic. While looking both ways is sound advice and may stop you from going into a road with a speeding car, ignoring or forgetting it isn't the actual cause of the accident.

Doing good causal analysis opens up our assumptions and leads to learning before jumping to a solution. (As usual, see The Toolbox for some handy help.)

Don't forget that the central function of Act is to maintain an intentional basis to do exactly that, including the whats and whys involved in such movement. When deciding what to act on, ask yourself: Will this action enable joy? Will it drive out fear? Will this action engage excellence?

Enabling joy and engaging excellence is what matters most. Project success and customer delight will naturally follow.

ACHIEVE

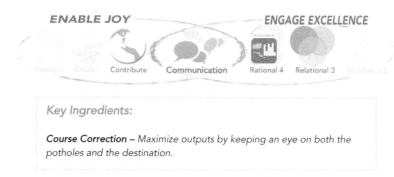

Key Ingredients:

Course Correction – Maximize outputs by keeping an eye on both the potholes and the destination.

Recall Deming's SIPOC model we talked about early on. Your team's Outputs – the tangible evidence of the project activity – are achieved due to their transformation of inputs.

One aspect of Outputs is the work itself, whether it's a new software package, a newly built house, an overhauled facility, a product campaign, a restored mission hospital… something you can see or use. The other aspect is the tangible data: what has been spent, what is still in the budget, when work was completed, quality checks, work completion reports, etc.

These achievements define how well you're satisfying the customer. They're evidence of meeting requirements, the budget and the schedule. These are the "what" of your project and the topics of your drumbeat meetings.

In Kano Model terms, these actions are what will minimize customer dissatisfaction, hopefully to nearly zero. Refer to the Kano tools in The Toolbox.

How does a project leader keep track of all the data concerning how well the project is being achieved? It's a project dashboard. That's a term that is overused, I know, but it's still in vogue for a reason.

Think of a dashboard in your car. It lets you know what the engine and drivetrain has done, along with our speed, engine health, miles and fuel left. Dashboards also now include a navigation system that lets you know estimated time of arrival and traffic conditions. Some even inform you of alternate routes: the "Refinable" part of CLEAR.

The science and discipline of minding and adjusting for what you learn from the project dashboard, known as project controls, is a field unto its own. So we won't cover it here. However, we do need to state that it isn't named very well.

It should instead be called a project navigation system. Because you need to know where to go next. That way, you're not spending your energy fretting over what happened yesterday. You need to tell your team what they're going to do tomorrow and next week.

As the information comes into the navigation system, and you see that money is flowing out faster than expected, yes. Of course. You'll need to make sure you don't have a hole in your money bag. However, the real question your team is looking to you to answer is what to do next. Using sentences that sound like, "You shouldn't have done that." provides very little insight on what to do next. Your job is to *lead* the project. Data and information from the dashboard merely tells you when, where and what to change, not how to lead that change.

Using our car metaphor again, you need to tell the team how fast to go, when to stop for gas, and what road to take; not tell them they went too fast, should've stopped earlier and should have taken that last exit.

That is why this element is called Achieve. It's a clear reminder that you lead the project's achievement. Yes, mistakes and bad decisions will occur. And in the Learn element, you'll see how we learn from them. For now though, you need to figure out how to navigate ahead.

ACCOMPLISH

Key ingredients:

Kano Model Delighters – *understanding and creating customer delight above and beyond customer satisfaction*

Deming's SIPOC model ends with C, which traditionally stands for Customer. But a better way to think about it is that it stands for outComes. After all, it is also the accomplishment, not just the achievement, that matters to the customer.

Project customers never only receive a product. They also receive a service experience.

Recall the Kano Model and the concept of delighters. Just like Achieve is the work of minimizing customer dissatisfaction, i.e. moving east on the lower Kano curve, Accomplish is moving northeast on the delighter curve.

How is a leader to do that? Let's re-visit our dashboard metaphor.

When you're driving your family on a long trip, is what you see on the dashboard the only indicator of trip excellence and joy? No, it's not. No doubt, we'll also have to use our rearview mirror a time or two to check if the kids in the back seat are okay.

Does the navigation system tell you how amazing the scenery is? How about the road condition? Where's the indicator that we're on a pothole-riddled, rattle-your-bones route? Does anything up there let you know that everyone's getting hungry and irritable? How about when to use a restroom? Does it tell us we're going through a dangerous area?

Obviously, the most important outCome of a trip is your arrival at the intended destination. But other outComes matter, such as whether the travelers got there happy and not in a state of frustration, exhaustion and exasperation.

Project controls provide you with a way to make sure you've got gas and oil to cover the miles. Enabling joy is about *Accomplishing* something of both tangible and intangible value.

It's not only making sure you've got the car ready for the trip, but making sure you arrive at your purposeful destination and that, with everyone involved feeling like it was a worthwhile venture that they'd want to do again. It's about maybe stopping for ice cream or having a blanket so that the non-driver doesn't mind a cool car that keeps the driver alert.

Or, remember the Tom Peters question before about what hotel you'd rather stay in; the one where employees loved their work or the one with a management goal of customer satisfaction. Enabling joy and delighting the customer work hand in hand.

The fruit of the enabling joy is that you set the expectation and promote the culture wherein the team sees, seizes, and fulfills opportunities that rely on human creativity, great customer connection and an empowered ability to contribute one's value and lead to delight. Remember that joy is strength: the strength to make the delight difference.

Achieving the project outputs is necessary. Of course. If you don't achieve satisfaction, it's nearly impossible to accomplish delight. However, in executing the project, you have those moments of interaction – even when something's gone wrong – where you can create customer delight. It's the classic creative spirit that can turn lemons into lemonade.

So what are the tools that complement the traditional project dashboard, letting you know how well your team is Accomplishing delightful outComes?

Hopefully, you now see that outComes are a human dimension, not one that's technical, financial or legal. To see how well your team is Accomplishing, you use the same tools you used in Dialogue, Discover and Encounter. You'll continue to go back to what you and your team did in Initiate to connect and build psychological safety. And you'll continue to rely on your team's Indoctrination to aspire to the vision you've set.

An idea to try: Kano proposed asking customers two almost identical questions about each feature: how would they feel if the feature were present, and how would they feel if the feature were absent. It may sound like overkill, but it's actually the combination of the two questions that make this a powerful technique.

For example, you might ask how the customer would feel if product demo videos were present. And they might answer, "I like it that way." Yet when you ask how they'd feel if product videos weren't present – they might say, "I expect it to be that way." This tells you they're an unexpected feature and therefore a delighter. Conversely, they might say, "I dislike it that way," meaning the feature is very much expected and they would like as many product videos as possible. This Kano Mapping is explained in detail in the Toolbox.

> *"Notice how I said 'leading,' not 'managing.' We have all the numbers and graphs we need to assess work management. What we were lacking was a way to assess how well we lead people. And we now have a way to do that."*
>
> *– From Enabling Joy*

Think It Through. Make It YOURS

1. Develop several ideas on how you'll make yourself less of a prisoner of the urgent.

2. Recall the metaphor about the metrics we have for taking a car trip. Do you have a plan to watch the good driver and content rider metrics as carefully as you do the miles driven and miles per gallon metrics?

3. Initiative from team members is a valuable commodity. However, as a leader, you'll need to continuously communicate the project scope so that team members will realize when they're creating value that isn't aligned with project goals.

    How will you manage a healthy balance between the two?

4. What evidence has your team seen of customer delight? Be specific. (e.g., what is the customer's mood at your drumbeat meetings with them?)

5. Look back at the steps you've learned, connecting them to how the various ones lead to either excellent achievement or joyful accomplishment of the project:

   a. **Invite** – Building on an asset mindset (i.e., "I can and want to do this project.")
   b. **Indoctrinate** – Presenting a vision that speaks to outcomes
   c. **Initiate** – Establishing trust so that everyone is "all in"
   d. **Dialogue** – Making sure we learn as a team
   e. **Discover** – Finding our limiting assumption
   f. **Define** – Putting together a CLEAR plan
   g. **Explore** – Ensuring good supply and mitigating risks
   h. **Encounter** – Testing as we go
   i. **Encourage** – Building the ability to perform under pressure.

   Are you confident that you've set your team up for success and your customer for satisfaction and delight?

6. What is your assessment of the goals set forth in Define in terms of CLEAR, especially Emotional, Appreciable, and Refinable? Do you see signs of the opposite of joy? (i.e., non-engagement, confusion, irrelevance, and/or compliance for compliance sake?)

7. Project work frequently ebbs and flows, with times of slack (*yes, that's an official project-scheduling word*) interspersed with crunch times that require extra hours. When your team is clouded by the extrinsic incentive (what Herzberg would call a 'dis-satisfier') called overtime, what is your plan to safeguard your people's morale and safety?

IDEAL: Lift up, Learn, Let go

At this point, the team members may want to say, "Whew!" The hurdles have been hopped, the customer satisfied and delighted. Is this the culmination of project joy?

Now that the team has con*tribute*d the project to its purpose, its owners and users, it's time to pay *tribute*: to recognize that they did it!

There is that, yes, but there's also more. You need to initiate the connections to what lays down the road, be it the next project or maybe using the project we just created.

For the people across The Relational Three, this means that we don't just wave goodbye to them. In the hectic world of projects, we too easily overlook the essential benefits of building bridges for connections to the next project and making sure we've increased our ability to create value towards future projects.

The IDEAL approach doesn't end with this project's delivery.

LIFT UP

ENABLE JOY   ENGAGE EXCELLENCE

Connect   Create   Contribute   Communication   Rational 4   Relational 3   Readiness 2

Key ingredients:

Thank – *Ensure the attitude of gratitude is fulfilled, person to person.*
Congratulate – *Recognize any heroic actions, unique and definable.*
Celebrate – *Make it communal, circling back to invite and initiate.*
Keep Track – *Stay true to every last detail.*

You've enabled the team to connect, create value and contribute. At this point, they've contributed, so it's time to pay tribute. You now need to develop an explicit plan to thank, congratulate and celebrate.

Thank: You Invited the team members, beginning an attitude of gratitude. This is where you have the opportunity to add specificity. Genuine thankfulness builds on joy, which enables connection. So this first part must be personal and specific. Otherwise it carries little meaning.

Thank people for the effort they put in and the choices they made, such as staying for late nights or weekends, not complaining about bad coffee, and making tough choices to uphold the team values.

Congratulate: Whereas you thank folks for their effort, you congratulate them for what they achieved or accomplished. Congratulating addresses the entire connect, create and contribute foundation of joy. In Latin, the word actually means to "share joy."

Like "thank you," it has to be linked to a specific outcome and addressed to a specific person or team. To do this, go back through early notes and documents – back in the I, D and E phases of the project. Look at some project team minutes to recall how deep in the valley of despair (i.e. storming) that group was compared to where they are now.

Stating a generic "we did a good job" or other similar blathering does not accomplish true sharing of joy.

Celebrate: This is the communal complement to the first two. This is the "Yeah, we did it!" time, where we throw our hats in the air. It's the bow on the package, connecting back to the initial team building events. It's communal and connective.

Celebrating the team's achievement is your opportunity to capstone the Initiate events that were your original steps to forming this team and the Indoctrinate steps that aligned the vision and values.

Keep Track: Even after handing off ownership of the project, you still need to have accountability and traceability for those remaining topics, open items and last-minute revisions that were agreed on. For this, use your Define tools.

LEARN

ENABLE JOY — ENGAGE EXCELLENCE

Connect   Create   Contribute   Communication   Rational 4   Relational 3   Readiness 2

Key Ingredients:

Retrospects – *These are explicit events where you should step back and apply the Study part of PDSA so that future projects can employ what your team learned in this one.*
Project Notes and Lessons – *Look them over to understand and create customer delight above and beyond customer satisfaction.*

The project seems over, but your calling to enable joy is not. Actually, you have an incredibly fertile area left to continue accomplishing that.

As we've seen, the components for joy are connecting, creating and contributing. And a key foundation for those is the discipline to seize the opportunities for learning. Why not take advantage of that when learning increases connection, and the ability to create and to see avenues for contribution.

Learning is a fundamentally joy-enabling process. To appreciate how deeply true this is, think of the joy toddlers have when they learn to walk or talk: how they seize every opportunity to learn what are actually the two most difficult tasks we humans figure out. You want to keep that sense of wonder, even at this final phase of the process.

The tendency, I know, is to clean out the office and move on. So you're going to need special amounts of discipline to push past that sense of absolute completion. Start with what you have:

- Have you conducted a rhythm of *After Action Reviews*? If so, pulling them together may reveal broader lessons about how to improve in the future.

- Have you conducted any *retrospects*? Consider conducting an end-of-project overall one. Many teams refer to events like retrospectives as post-mortems. (I've even heard of the term "pre-mortems" before.) But you and your team are bringing a project to life, not killing something. So make sure your language is consistent with enabling joy and engaging excellence instead.

- Have you embedded a *journalist* or kept a diary? This is the time to use them. If you implemented this idea, now is the time to read the novel. This would best be done by the whole team, with an opportunity to do a "book club" dialogue when everything else is said and done.

- Conduct a post-project *review with the stakeholders and/or contractors*. This also helps to establish closure to the teaming you've engendered throughout the project.

In short, the goal of this element is to not waste the learning that may still be on the table. You want to absorb it all in order to better engage excellence in future projects; to help all team members grow in their ability to connect, create and contribute; and to put closure to those many instances where people are still wondering, "Should we have done such and such?"

LET GO

ENABLE JOY ———————— ENGAGE EXCELLENCE

Connect   Create   Contribute   Communication   Rational 4   Relational 3   Readiness 2

> *Key ingredients:*
>
> **Referrals and Recommendations** – *The ones who contributed deserve to be set up for future joy.*
> **Resume Builders** — *Always return people better than you received them.*

The project is now complete. The customer has the keys, the user manual and the warranty certificate.

As such, you and the team are standing back to take a proud look at the completed project. As leader, your role for enabling joy now comes full circle.

Is this the end? Yes. This time, it really is. But because this is a monumental change (i.e., the end of the project life, the disbanding of the project team), you still have a big role to fulfill.

Remember: Leaders lead change.

You need to enable your team to be able to connect to a future project and your contractors to a future contract. You need to ensure the relevancy of people's ability to create value and the expectation of future opportunities for them to contribute that value. This is the phase where you prepare for the next project – by you or by anyone else on the team.

- **For your team members**: Make explicit how their contributions have made them more valuable, more responsible, better prepared to lead and ready for broader range of tasks. Ask them to update their resumes, and help them to describe how their contributions will enable them to be better at creating value on future projects or in other organizational positions.

  Have a frank conversation about how you saw their talents and how you invested them in enabling joy or engaging excellence to grow those talents into strengths.

- **For temporary team members and contractors**: For those who have contracts that expire at the project's end, conduct conversations to help them have safe landings into other opportunities or to provide a ready reference. One way to do this is to investigate how you can provide testimonials they can use in their marketing efforts.

- **For your trusted suppliers**: Help them be a readily available supplier on future projects as well. Take the time to provide references, referrals or testimonials. Tell your peer project managers about them.

As a last part of Let Go, you yourself need to be ready to retire your identity as leader of this project team. You need to respectfully realize that you are now relieved of command, so to speak. The project is operational. So celebrate!
It's a wise practice to schedule some time away – a vacation – at this point, and not rush into the next project. You need time to recharge and reflect on the experience and how it has helped you grow.

Think It Through. Make It YOURS

1. What is your plan for thanking each participant? For those you asked to Contribute and who HAVE contributed, do you have a plan to pay tribute?

2. What is your plan for celebrating project completion?

3. For contractors, describe your plan to provide recommendations for them based on their work in this project. Has your relationship with them on this project increased their ability to succeed as contractors?

4. What is your plan to maintain commitment for those little tasks that may exist after project completion: the touch-up and tuning work that team members want to just brush off?

5. What is your plan to record and store the documents that now are the storyline of this action movie you called a project?

6. For the customer and stakeholders, have you asked them for their constructive feedback? Have you developed an opportunity for a session to share what was learned to better lead future projects?

7. What is your plan to capture the excellent practices or procedures your team believes were foundational to being IDEAL?

The IDEAL Approach
Idea to Real
Enabling Joy
Engaging Excellence

Lift up
Learn
L Let go

Act
Achieve
A Accomplish

Explore
Encounter
E Encourage

I Invite
Initiate
Indoctrinate **D** Dialogue
Discover
Define

ENABLE JOY

ENGAGE EXCELLENCE

Connect   Create   Contribute   Communication   Rational 4   Relational 3   Readiness 2

Strengthen Your Epic

How's your movie shaping up?

The IDEAL approach is a template to direct and make your epic ideal: to transform an idea into a reality with joy and excellence. Your epic movie will not move neatly from beginning to end. But by mentally preparing and making it personal via the IDEAL approach in this book, you can direct day-to-day responses to the twists and turns.

You should now see how the various elements feed and reinforce each other. By starting with gratitude in Invite, you'll be able to neatly wrap up the project with a sincere thanks in Lift Up. It will be more of a natural act whose stage was set from the get-go.

By Initiating, you've established psychological safety, laying a critical cornerstone for Dialogue, Discover, Explore, Encounter and Learn.

By Indoctrinating, you set the ability to not only Achieve, but – even more importantly – to Accomplish.

Moving to the D phase (Dialogue, Discover and Define), you built the critical building blocks of the Rational Four and Relational Three; establishing tangible touchpoints and processes for Connect and Create.

The E steps, meanwhile, were the transition from planning to doing, building on what you created with I and D and preparing your team for A and L. With Encounter, you conducted intentional testing to make sure that your plans, assumptions and prototypes wouldn't blindside anyone due to the team's tunnel-vision focus on making progress.

This then laid a sturdier foundation to Act, Achieve and Accomplish. With Encourage, you reinforce your team's ability to connect, create and contribute with specific plans that deal with the pressure the A juncture will bring.

In L, Lift up, Learn and Let Go are the exit strategies that complement the careful team building and project achievement. They preserve the fruits of joyful connection, creation and contribution and enable future engaging for excellence.

Leading is personal. Joy is strength.

Think It Through. Make It YOURS

1. What have been your biggest learning moments (those a-ha moments) for leading an IDEAL project?

2. Which parts of the IDEAL approach are you feeling uncomfortable or doubtful about? Do you have a plan or strategy that you will use instead of the IDEAL approach for that part?

3. Do you have questions about the IDEAL approach? I recommend asking the author.

The Toolbox

Quick-use templates and guides for the various tools and techniques that have been mentioned to help you lead the IDEAL project.

Advocacy and Inquiry Guidelines

Why Use: To understand and become better at the two basic roles in a conversation.

When to Use: Best when taught during the formation of the project team. Should be refreshed and used throughout the lifecycle of the project.

Advocacy is a skillful conversation tool wherein we invite others to test our own assumptions to better understand d and improve our assumptions.
Inquiry is a skillful conversation tool wherein we openly invite others to express their views and develop a better understanding of their assumptions.

As the team explores the everchanging issues of the project, advocacy and inquiry are key learning tools that increase our understanding of all team members' view and perspectives. This key communication skill promotes the team ability to engage excellence, enable joy and delight the customer.

**There is rarely an argument over the facts,
just the assumptions around the facts.**

"We spent half the budget in only one quarter of the time; this is really bad."
In this quote, notice that the only facts are that half the budget was spent and in one quarter of the time. Since assumptions tacked onto facts are not facts, here's two quick rules of thumb:

1. If it's a prediction, it's probably an assumption. By and large, we are not perfect prophets.
2. If it's an adjective, it's frequently an assumption about how we're seeing the facts.

A Guide for Skillful Advocacy

TAG Note: These steps are considered universal, but you should ensure cultural fit and appropriateness.

Step	Guidance	What it sounds like:
State your assumptions	Describe how your interpretation of the data led to those assumptions.	"Here's what I see…I assumed that…?"
Explain your assumptions.	Tell the story that you believe the facts are telling you.	"We spent half the budget. I think we will run out of money if we are not more frugal."
Explain your context.	Share why this is important to you and why your perspective if of value to others.	"I am nervous we will run short and not be able to keep our promise."
Encourage others to test your assumption,	Ask them share how they'd do it, to poke holes in your story; how the data speaks differently to them…	"What do you think…"
Reveal where you are least clear in understanding the meaning of the data	Candidly expose where the facts don't directly support your assumptions	"I know we've been in this position before and we made it, but…."
Refrain from defensiveness	Show you are open to getting a better understanding.	"'I'm accountable to the customer for this, but then again, I don't want to be a Chicken Little."

A Guide for Skillful Inquiry

TAG Note: These steps are considered universal, but you should ensure cultural fit and appropriateness.

Step	Guidance	What it sounds like:
Search for their assumptions	Gently move back to the data. Find out how they arrived at their assumption.	*"What leads you to conclude that?"* *"What data supports that?"*
Show that you need help understanding their point of view	Remember that you may not understand, not that their assumption is wrong.	*"Can you help me understand your thinking here?"* *"When I see this data, I don't come to the same assumption."*
Draw their reasoning.	You might want to draw it physically to help everyone see it better, including the owner.	
Test what is said by putting it another way or in another context,	Use metaphors or simulations.	*"Would this be like…"*
Explore the boundaries of the reasoning	Where does the assumption break down?	*"I agree with your need to… but I don't agree with your…."*
Try contrasting	The if – then approach	*"If that is true, then will this…also be true?"*

After Action Review

Why Use: To have an intentional method for learning while in the flow of work in order to raise accountability of incremental improvements; excellent for instilling a rhythm of learning.

When to Use: During any phase, but especially during execution following a defined, short-duration task.

An **After Action Review (AAR)** is a structured conversation with the intent to learn from today to improve for tomorrow. The people who participated in the event are the analysts, no one else. And any leader who provided the immediate directions for the event is considered a participant.

This provides for accountability and eliminates the effect of outsiders. The team analyzes what happened – not what could, should or might have happened. They compare what did happen with what they expected to happen. And they look at what happened that was unexpected, both good, bad and indifferent.

In short, an AAR is the Study part of the Plan-Do-Study-Act process, comparing outputs and outcomes with the team's planned intent.

Notice how an AAR isn't the typical de-brief. It is only the participants amongst themselves taking note of what's been going on to help with system thinking and future problem solving. If the AAR produces recommendations to improving tomorrow, these must be for the participants themselves, not for outsiders or others. AAR's need to be done immediately, within hours of the event.

Facilitators may be helpful in running an AAR, in which case you should think of using them as a way to kickstart the team's ability to do them on their own.

To help your team, consider pre-printing these three questions on a sheet or pad of paper that team members can jot down notes on. This will allow them to think, recall and then write without first being distracted by another person's observations. There is NO intent to collect these papers.

After Action Review
Cue Card

Here's what I thought we intended to do.

Here's what I expected.

Here's what happened.

Here's what I saw that I didn't expect.

Leading the IDEAL Project

Causal Analysis Diagram

Why Use: To clarify the complexities in understanding the causes behind both undesirable and desirable outputs or outcomes.

When to Use: Any time where the team needs to learn from unexpected results to improve future performance, especially in Encounter and Learn elements.

How to Use: Act like a four-year-old and ask "why, why, why, why, why."

Using a big whiteboard or some butcher paper on a table, guide the team to keep asking why, starting at the event and then working backwards in time or causation. Put each suggested cause on a note. Ideally, you'll start at the right side, with a statement of the problem, and then work to the left, unpacking each cause at a time. It rarely works that neatly. Expect to move notes around. Many causes are long standing. Many will need to be moved as they won't get mentioned in their order of causation. By flexibly recording the team's ideas, you can maintain team input and continually refine the order of the causes. This will help preclude paralysis by analysis and maintain energy.

Asking "why" at least five layers deep is recommended. (It's actually a well-known causal analysis technique called, shockingly, the Five Whys.)

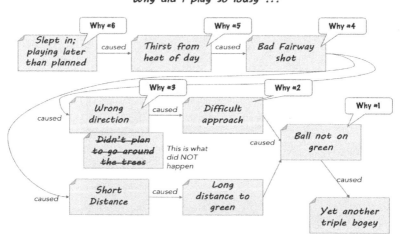

Why did I play so lousy ?!?

Helpful Rules of Causal Analysis:

Rule #1: ONLY state what's happened, not what has NOT happened. This sounds obvious, but it's not. Lots of times, you'll hear someone say something like "because we didn't have supervision, we didn't have a risk plan" or "we didn't have a good estimate." These are "missing possible solutions" not causes. Lack of a fire extinguisher never caused a fire. (see how we didn't allow that in the example above)

Rule #2: Differentiate multiple causes from chain reactions. For instance, fire needs three causes: air, heat and fuel. A chain reaction could then be: the plastic on stove caught fire, that caused cabinet to burn, then kitchen.

Rule #3: Map it from right to left. That way, when you're done, it reads left to right from initial cause(s) to final effect.

Rule #4: Expect parallel causes; there is rarely a root cause. For most events, there's a combination of causes that have aligned somehow. Some causes may have occurred years ago and weren't recognized as such until other causes came along. (e.g. papers were put in the attic years ago; faulty wiring has been an ongoing issue, but just recently we overloaded the circuit to cause the papers to ignite.)

Often, many of the causes are system effects that get worse over time (e.g., bad leader behavior causing non-joy, fear gradually goes up, people do the minimum and don't engage excellence).

Rule #5: Stop when the cause is human behavior (e.g., "I forgot" or "I didn't know"). We never really know the causes to human behavior. Don't let folks start listing the missing solution as the cause, see Rule #1.

> **TAG NOTE:**
> For events that occur across time zones, it's critical to keep the sequence of events clearly noted, since your morning may be a teammate's night.

CLEAR Goals

Why Use: To maintain team cohesiveness and passion in balance with pragmatic project requirements.

When to Use: In the Initiate and Define elements. Also, whenever project team members or objectives change. CLEAR goals are designed to work with the dynamic, ever-changing nature of the project lifecycle. Each CLEAR aspect particularly supports IDEAL elements as noted.

Collaborative: Goals encourage team engagement and the ability to connect, create and contribute to project excellence.
IDEAL elements: Invite, Initiate, Dialog, Define, Encourage.

Limited: Concisely define each goal with a timeframe to keep it fresh.
IDEAL elements: Define, Act, Achieve, Accomplish.

Emotional: Each goal not only addresses the pragmatic realities of project excellence, but also builds belief in its contribution to delighting the customer and igniting team joy.
IDEAL elements: Invite, Indoctrinate, Encounter, Encourage, Lift-Up

Appreciable: Goals build upon each other, allowing the team to understand them as connectable milestones toward the team vision.
IDEAL elements: Define, Explore, Encounter, Encourage, Act.

Refinable: Provide flexibility to allow modifying your goals to build in a continual ability to increase customer delight, project excellence or team joy.
IDEAL elements: Explore, Achieve, Accomplish, Lift-Up, Learn.

CLEAR goals reinforce the components of enabling joy, engaging excellence and communicating. By design, they are a continually revisited set of goals the team aligns to – while also recognizing the need to learn and adapt as the project progresses.

CLEAR goals are NOT the same as the familiar SMART goals that have been used in business for years. As a refresh, SMART stands for:

- **Specific** – Goals are clear and unambiguous.

- **Measurable** – Results can be measured in some way, such as the percentage increase in sales or the number of employees trained.

- **Attainable** – Goals are realistic and attainable by the average worker.

- **Relevant** – Goals relate to your organization's vision and mission.

- **Time-bound** – Goals have definite starting and ending points, and a fixed duration.

SMART goals are good for incremental changes that you want to control. They are not as useful when capitalizing on the chaos of human creativity or the inherent changeable dynamics of taking an idea and transforming it into reality.

Drumbeat Agenda Template

Why Use: To maintain a certain steadying rhythm that holds true during the inevitable changes in the flavor, loading and pace of the project workload through the project lifecycle.

When to Use: At the beginning of the project.

Duration (minutes - overall 30)	Topic (align with IDEAL)	Caster (person who plans and casts the topic out)
10	Check In Gratefulness Update...	Project Leader
5	Safety Share	Project Leader
15	How Yesterday went - PDSA	Project Leader Ops Leader
15	Eisenhower Box	Planner/Scheduler
10	Supplier Update	Buyer
5	Send Off	Project Leader
	Post Drumbeat Special Topic	
20	Dialog on a single topic. This timeslot would be reserved prior to or during the drumbeat. This is designed to provide a reserved spot for issues that need deeper thinking. (note: this should not always be needed)	

Eisenhower Box

Why Use: To help calm chaos when urgency hijacks importance, misaligning priorities. Or to make sense of expected actions in the heat of the battle.

When to Use: Anytime the team seems overwhelmed by actions and tasks that "have to be done yesterday" and/or there's a sense of confused chaos in getting through hectic and long days.

The Eisenhower Box is a template to perhaps permanently put on a whiteboard. That way, during Drumbeat meetings, you can put tasks into their respective quadrants to maintain visibility and generate discussion.

This classification can create joy, helping you clarify where to channel your energy to best connect, create value and contribute to excellence. It can also provide clarity when the team is struggling to prioritize work. The hidden value of the Eisenhower Box is that it serves as a subliminal reminder to be proactive – that the team is not the victim of the project.

Eisenhower Box Template

	Urgent	**Not Urgent**
Important	**DO** Do It Now (*e.g., See customer about issue, Drumbeat*)	**DECIDE** Plan When to Do It (*e.g., Conduct morale booster; Write reference*)
Not Important	**DELEGATE** Find Someone to Do It (*e.g., Go through emails*)	**DELETE** Eliminate It (*e.g., Sign off trip reports*)

Influence Mapping

Why Use: To help your project team understand the complex interplay of customer, stakeholder and sponsor organizations in order to maximize the effectiveness of communications.

When to Use: When the team believes they're meeting roadblocks.

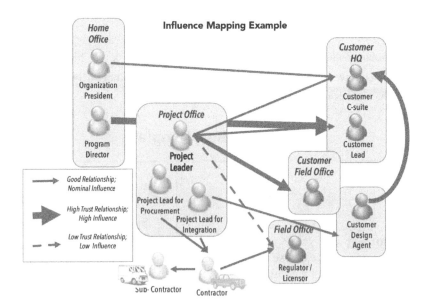

Journaling

Why Use: To develop a project history that promotes an understanding of causal factors that led to the success or failure of project events.

When to Use: Throughout the project lifecycle.

Journaling can take several forms, from a simple daily diary maintained by key members of the team… to amalgamating project correspondence… to employing a professional writer. There are merits and downsides to each.

The diary approach maintains the best first-person perspective on issues, actions, decisions and outcomes. But it also taxes people's time, particularly those people with the least to give. And it relies heavily on the diary keepers to have very good notetaking skills.

Meanwhile, compiling project correspondences (e.g., letters, texts, emails, blog postings, tweets), it does require curating, which may be a time-intensive endeavor.

As for employing an embedded journalist, it offers several advantages: single point of view, a level of objective observation, an ability to capture events in prose and a consistent writing style. The downside is the cost of this embedded journalist.

This is where some creative approaches may come in handy. Perhaps offer this position to someone studying technical communications or even creative writing as an externship or internship. Or contact a professional publication so as to create a real-time case study.

Regardless, it's not necessarily valuable to assign a journalist who's incredibly knowledgeable about the project's technical aspects since the IDEAL project is balanced across project and people dimensions. Focus more on having one who's keenly observant of human behavior, acutely listens to conversations – both what is said and what isn't – and trustworthy enough that everyone feels comfortable giving him or her free passage to what's going on with who.

Kano Model

Why Use: To set the stage on why just satisfying the customer is only part of the project objectives – why we also want to interconnect enabling joy with customer delight.

When to Use: During concept and team development.

The Kano Model was developed by Noriaki Kano and built off the work of Frederick Herzberg's motivational model. In essence, what Herzberg reveals about our team, Kano reveals about our customers.

Its usefulness is in the simple graphic it offers to help differentiate satisfying customers versus delighting them. It paints the picture that meeting the requirement is a given in order to not dissatisfy customers, but how the best that goal will produce is satisfied customers. In other words, they got no more than what they paid for.

In the Kano Model, it's easy to think in terms of three types of customer needs: basic, performance and excitement (or delight). These are detailed in the next tool on using the Kano Model. However, you need to lay a foundation for the concepts here:

- **Basic needs** – Cost, schedule, scope, safety, legal.
- **Performance needs** – What you need to get it done with a competent team that the customer can work with. The more competent and easier to work with, the better.
- **Excitement needs** – Those needs that, if unfulfilled, won't dissatisfy the customer but, when they're filled, are game changers.

Take a look at the Kano Models. Figure 1 is an all-purpose Kano. Figure 2 is a project-oriented Kano. Take note of these key takeaways:

- Delight and Satisfaction are pursued concurrently, but not with the same approach.
- The dynamics of satisfying the customer is the process of diminishing returns. You can't really satisfy beyond being in budget, on time and per contract.
- It's easy to slip down the satisfier slope with late delivery, blown budgets or sloppy quality.
- The dynamics of delighting a customer is expansive; there is no logical limit to how much you can delight them.
- Having a team that can delight a customer relies on the same enablers that enable joy. That is the strength that joy provides: the strength to delight.

Figure 1

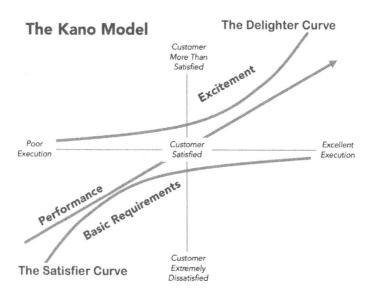

Figure 2

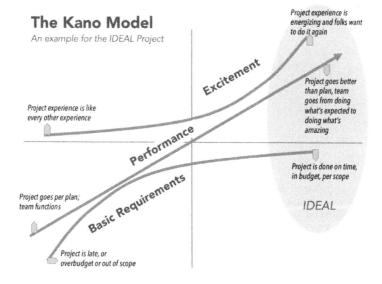

Kano Model Mapping

Why Use: To better understand customer needs in context of requirements and delighters, and to interconnect joy and excellence for the customer.

When to Use: During concept development and when exploring ideas for changes or revisions to the current plan.

To help clarify whether certain features are required or all delighters, consider the following graphic.

- For each feature (design change, idea, recommendation), ask:
If this feature is absent, I would _____ it.
- For each feature (design change, idea, recommendation), ask:
If this feature is present, I would _____ it.

Like   Expect   Wouldn't Notice   Live with   Dislike

Make sure that, for each feature, you score both the upside of it being present and the downside of it being absent. Something that has little upside but a lot of downside is a must-have and should be provided. Something with a lot of upside and no downside is a delighter and could be done, but isn't mandatory.

This helps to clarify whether certain actions by the project team will drive toward excellence or joy. The emphasis that you need to have as a leader has to be balanced between responsive and proactive: enabling excellence and enabling joy.

The graphic below uses the clarifying insight of the Kano Model as a template to help identify how various leadership actions, all of them valuable, need to be balanced.

Look at your calendar. How much time and energy are you putting into each of these leadership actions? Your real priority is revealed by where you put your time and money.

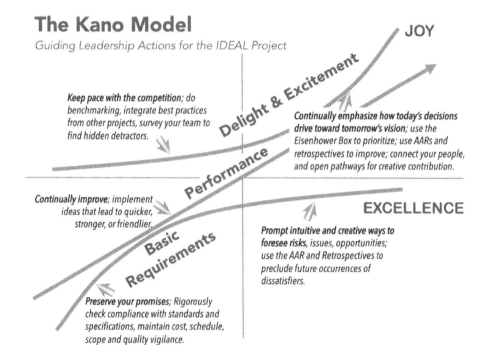

The Kano Model
Guiding Leadership Actions for the IDEAL Project

JOY

Delight & Excitement

Keep pace with the competition; do benchmarking, integrate best practices from other projects, survey your team to find hidden detractors.

Continually emphasize how today's decisions drive toward tomorrow's vision; use the Eisenhower Box to prioritize; use AARs and retrospectives to improve; connect your people, and open pathways for creative contribution.

Performance

Continually improve; implement ideas that lead to quicker, stronger, or friendlier.

EXCELLENCE

Basic Requirements

Prompt intuitive and creative ways to foresee risks, issues, opportunities; use the AAR and Retrospectives to preclude future occurrences of dissatisfiers.

Preserve your promises; Rigorously check compliance with standards and specifications, maintain cost, schedule, scope and quality vigilance.

LEAD THE **IDEAL** PROJECT • 161

Perform Under Pressure

Why Use: To help people tap those human capacities that allow them to perform when situations cause pressure and tasks are most critical or urgent.

When to Use: During the Act part of a project, when many tasks are under tight budget and time constraints, and people start to feel the heat.

There's no secret sauce to performing under pressure. To be the project leader you need to be, you must enliven your team's adaptive skills – which are already part of the human psyche. Here is an easy to remember tool that provides a quick summary of those skills.

Engage your better self– A Pause matters
Relieve the pressure – Believe what matters
Unhijack your neocortex – Simulate the possible
Strap on your training – Rely on what you can do
Step out - Marine Corps!
Excite possibility – Think greatness, not failure
Reframe – It's a challenge to live up to, not a test
PERFORM

<u>**Engage your better self**</u> – **A pause matters:** Many times, pressure is caused by a sense of urgency fueled by pressing time constraints. When our emotions sense this impending "not on time" crisis, it triggers an emotional response known as an amygdala hijack. The hijack is an actual neuro-chemical process wherein the emotional brain sends a signal to the thinking brain to shut down in an effort to save energy so as to fight, flight or freeze.

Science shows that taking a pause reduces the likelihood of that happening. Many of us have learned the "count to 10" tactic when we feel ourselves get upset. And that actually has a scientific basis.

So when your team feels the pressure, coach them to take a pause that matters and to allow their thinking brain to engage their better self.

Relieve the pressure – **Believe what matters:** There is important, and there is urgent. Many events in project life are urgent and therefore seem important. By using the Eisenhower Box (also in The Toolbox) you can help your team keep what's most important at the forefront. Sometimes, it's a matter of reminding them that they're all safe and that the current crisis is resolvable.

This is why vision, mission and values are so critical. They're what really matter.

Unhijack your neocortex – **Simulate the possible**: Pressure mounts when we only see the problems. Again, this tactic attempts to kickstart the thinking brain and negate the effect of an amygdala hijack.

As a leader, you need to lead the team into thinking of solutions, not laundry listing all the problems and issues. When the conversation can't seem to find a solution, invert the problem statement, asking such questions as 1) "If this problem were magically solved overnight, how would we know?" 2) "What DO we have that is working?" 3) "What solution do we have that only requires us to have more courage?"

Strap on your training – **Rely on what you can do:** Similar to the tactic above, this is good for pressure that's based in a physical activity, such as working with electrical equipment or dealing with medical, fire and other emergencies. It's also the same tactic used by first responders and the military. By heavily training their people, the training takes over when the situation is pressure filled.

You need to continually coach your team by first making sure they have been trained and then reminding them to "do what you've been trained to do."

There's a classic scene in the move *Hidden Figures* where a black female mathematician needs to solve a problem in front of a crowd of skeptical, white, male engineers. She whispers to herself that "the math never fails you" and straps on her math training to power through the pressure filled moment.

Step out – **Marine Corps!:** This is a way to reduce the pressure triggering the emotional fear of being alone. As explained earlier in the book, this tactic is based on a common technique Marines use to teach recruits parachuting. When they're at the door scared to jump, they've been taught to say out loud (so it's more real to their senses) "Marine Corps," reminding them that they're not alone in the jump: that they have the Marine Corps serving them and that they are serving the Marines.

When you have a team member who's under pressure and starting to feel like he or she is on the proverbial windy corner, remind her or him that they have a team.

<u>Excite possibility</u> – **Think greatness, not failure**: This is where you need to draw on your asset thinking and to continually focus the team on the solutions and the outcome of the solutions, not the effect of the failure. Similar to many sports coaching techniques, it's about picturing the possible against all odds.

Enabling the team to focus on what they need to do to be great is a creativity-enabling mindset. Whereas having them dwell on what they need to do to not fail triggers emotional reactions.

<u>Reframe</u> – **It's a challenge to live up to, not a test**: The notion of failing is a common cause of pressure. Failing in view of others triggers fear of being alone, of being rejected and of being discounted – basically the opposites of connect, create and contribute.

As leader, you need to pull your team beyond the remedy and re-focus them on the vision. This has to be more than generic cheerleading. You need to show how the right answer to today's crisis will define how they delight their customer.

This can be the crucible moment of this project epic.

PICK Chart

Why Use: To categorize and prioritize a list of desired or suggested ideas, in-
itiatives or solutions based on their return on investment ROI; or, put simply,
to get the most bang for their buck.

When to Use: Anytime that a list of options is developed.

Figure 1 (below) is the simple approach that aligns with the acronym PICK.

Figure 1

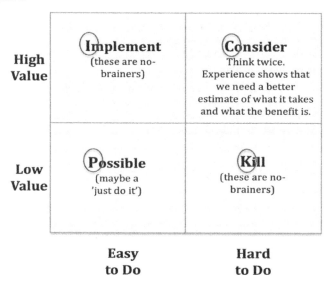

Figure 2 (next page)is an example of a more granular approach that helps
the team add some level of clarity to the terms Low and High.

The PICK tool works very well when you define a quantum leap from each level (e.g. weeks to months to years). Doing this reduces the tendency of teams to get paralysis by analysis, disagreeing on what high and low mean, or trying to be unnecessarily precise in time or effort estimates.

These levels are only an example. You need to define gradations that are appropriate to your project.

Figure 2

	Man-weeks to do	Man-months to do	Man-years to do
Earns Hundreds of Thousands of Dollars	**Do First**	**Do Second**	**Re-evaluate or Re-define**
Earns Tens of Thousands of Dollars	**Do Second or Third**	**Do or Leave**	**Don't Do; Kill**
Earns Thousands of Dollars	**Do or Leave**	**Don't Do; Kill**	**Don't Do; Kill**

PLAN-DO-STUDY-ACT (PDSA aka PDCA)

Why Use: To maintain clarity on distinct steps to achieve learning in the course of doing a project.

When to Use: Across the entire project lifecycle.

PDSA, the Plan-Do-Study-Act cycle, is an iterative method to enable control and continuous improvement of the project processes. It's known as the Deming circle/cycle/wheel, even though Deming called it the Shewhart cycle. It has its foundation in the familiar scientific method – the one defined by Francis Bacon in the 1600s: hypothesis, experiment, evaluate.

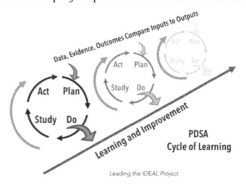

Leading the IDEAL Project

Plan – Establish what you expect to be the results, outputs and outcomes of a given project goal or milestone.

Do – Execute the plan on a small basis, a pilot or with some baby steps.

Study (or Check) – Gather the evidence of how the "Do" transpired. Get objective results, and compare the actual output with the desired and planned output. Decide if this is what's needed.

Act (and/or Adjust) – Based on "Study." If the results were not ideal, modify your approach (inputs or the process itself) and set in motion another PDSA cycle. If the results were ideal, and the process is stable (not just a one-time stroke of luck), move forward with the Plan.

RACI

Why Use: To clarify the roles and responsibilities, especially defining the person accountable for various tasks, phases and deliverables of the project.

When to Use: At the start of the project lifecycle (in the Define element)and whenever there's a notable change in plan or team membership.

Example for an IDEAL Project	Susan Program Director	Lucy Project Leader	Edmund Chief Designer	Peter Field Office Leader	Digory Customer Lead
Initiating	A	R	C	I	C
Planning	C	A/R	R	C	I
Executing	I	A/R	C	R	I
Testing	I	C	C	A/R	I
Closing Out	A	R	C	C	R

R – The person(s) **RESPONSIBLE** for doing the work; often more than one person.

A – The ONE person who holds the final **ACCOUNTABILITY** of the work, the money, the plan. The signature at the bottom of the page.
Many times, the ACCOUNTABLE person is also RESPONSIBLE.

C – Persons who are **CONSULTED** for their input, advice, or counsel BEFORE there is a decision to move forward.

I – Person(s) who are **INFORMED** after the decision is made so as to be aware, follow, know status, etc.

Relationship Mapping

Why Use: To clarify who should be intentionally building rapport with whom to maintain tight relationships critical to project and team communication.

When to Use: Best to develop at the beginning of the project.

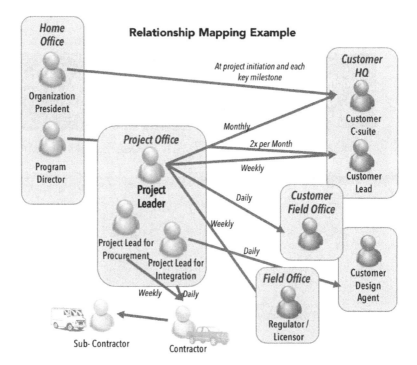

Retrospective

Why Use: To learn from major evolutions in the project lifecycle in order to improve the remainder of the project or future projects.

When to Use: After key events or milestones during the course of the project.

Retrospectives are learning events that are typically more formal than AARs. They're the opportunity to improve major processes for the rest of the current project or, more likely, for future projects. While AARs are tactical by design, retrospectives need to be strategic in nature.

Retrospectives are not opportunities to do causal analyses. If unexpected or undesired outputs or outcomes were realized, a dedicated causal analysis should be performed. Retrospectives need to be forward-focused, since the emphasis is on the Study and Act parts of the PDSA learning cycle.

Retrospectives, like AARs, are *learning* events, not blame finding events. They do not excuse accountability to our decisions and actions, but the purpose at this point is to improve for the future, not pay retribution for the past.

In addition, retrospectives are best performed when they focus on one phase of the project. However, looking across an entire project lifecycle with an end of project retrospective can reveal how early decisions and actions impacted later project activities.

Retrospective
Template

P
l
a
n
What did we plan or intend to happen?

What were the Expected results?

D
o
What were the Unexpected results?

S
t
u
d
y
What adjustments did we make and how effective were they?

Define the newly learned proven practice:

A
c
t
How will we ensure that this learning is retained and implemented?

Leading the IDEAL Project

Risk and Opportunity Analysis

Why Use: To aid in explicitly addressing, dialoguing, agreeing and aligning on the dimensions, actions and priorities of identified risks and opportunities.

When to Use: Anytime during the project lifecycle, however, it is most valuable in the Explore element.

If you have an initial collection, say a brainstorm, of risks and/or opportunities, then you want to use the Risk Matrix and/or the Opportunity Matrix. It's best to reproduce these templates on a big surface, whiteboard, chalkboard or easel pad, and then have the team put sticky notes on identifying how they see each risk or opportunity on the Likelihood and Impact scales. The template matrix then provides an initial suggestion on the actions for the team to take.

While the Risk Matrix allows you to prioritize, it is missing a dimension, that of detectability. When looking at risks that seem difficult to mitigate, you should think about using the Risk of Failure template. This tool is intended to enable taking a deeper look at identified risks. The items can range from a failed estimate, to a failed contractor or supplier; the items can also be possible events along the way that you and your team want to at least be prepared for. This tool can get tedious when teams get painstakingly precise in the scoring. Recommend that you first decide if such preciseness is necessary. Many times, just using thumb rule scoring provides the insight, learning that the team needs to identify and take effective action.

Risk Template (Matrix)

You can define your own levels; be specific to the needs of team and project

Impact (Severity)

Likelihood (Probability)	Inconvenient (No injury, minor schedule or financial impact)	Minor	Recoverable (Cause human harm, financial hardship, Customer loss)	Major	Irrecoverable (Fatal, Catastrophic, Financial Ruin)
Almost certain — Very likely to occur, but it's not a given.	Be Aware	Have a Plan	Have a Plan	Must Resolve	Must Resolve
Likely	Be Aware	Be Aware	Have a Plan	Must Resolve	Must Resolve
Possible — May occur at some time; within the reasonable realm of possibility	Low Priority	Be Aware	Be Aware	Have a Plan	Must Resolve
Unlikely	Low Priority	Low Priority	Be Aware	Be Aware	Have a Plan
Rare — Could, but probably will never happen	Low Priority	Low Priority	Low Priority	Be Aware	Have a Plan

This area typically shown as 'green.'

This area typically shown as 'yellow.'

This area typically shown as 'red.'

This is best used when the team has developed a list of potential risks so that the team can then plot them in relation to each other and prioritize which ones to act on.

Opportunity Template (Matrix)

Benefit (Advantage)

You can define your own levels; be specific to the needs of team and project

Likelihood (Probability)

		Good Idea (Saves 1000's of dollars or mandays; improves safety)	Stop & Think	Great Idea (Saves tens of thousands of $'s or manweeks; eliminate safety concern)	Amazing	Game Changer (Changes the game for the customer; yields delight)
Very likely to occur, but it's not a given.	**Almost certain**	Stay Tuned	Give it a try; pilot	Give it a try; pilot	Go !	Go !
	Likely	Stay Tuned	Stay Tuned	Give it a try; pilot	Go !	Go !
May occur at some time; within the reasonable realm of possibility	**Possible**	Re-check the ROI	Stay Tuned	Stay Tuned	Give it a try; pilot	Go !
	Unlikely	Re-check the ROI	Re-check the ROI	Stay Tuned	Stay Tuned	Give it a try; pilot
Could, but probably will never happen	**Rare**	Re-check the ROI	Re-check the ROI	Re-check the ROI	Stay Tuned	Give it a try; pilot

This is best used when the team has developed a list of improvements, productivity boosters, customer delighters, or new discoveries so that the team can then plot them in relation to each other and prioritize which ones to act on.

Risk of Failure Template (Matrix)

System, process, or specific work item	What could go wrong	Impact	Score 1-9	Likelihood	Score 1-9	Detectability	Score 1-9	Overall Score (Multiply 3 scores)	What you will do
	Describe WHAT might happen	*Describe HOW MUCH it will hurt*	*	*Describe WHEN or in what situation might happen*	*	*Describe HOW you can see it coming*	*	*Work on biggest scores first*	*Describe how the action reduces the risk; changes the scores*
	Continue to include all concerns, giving each concern the same analysis.								

This is best used when the team has developed a list of concerns and you want to include ALL THREE dimensions of risk, and evaluate across them with rigor.
* To do this, you need to develop a standard set of what the score numbers mean so that the whole team can similarly connect with this process and be aligned in creating value to identifying, classifying, ranking and working on reducing risks.

SIPOC

Why Use: To clarify the fundamental work process by understanding what is needed going in and what the transformation of those inputs will produce in terms of outputs and outcomes. Similarly, to think in reverse (COPIS) on what it will take to achieve desired outputs or accomplish desired outcomes.

When to Use: As a fundamental backdrop to work-planning and team-learning.

Supply   **I**nputs   **P**rocess **(Transformation)**   **O**utputs   **C**ustomer Out**C**ome

Person/Organization that provides the raw goods   What is needed to enable the Process   Where the real value happens; transforming inputs into outputs   The tangible items that are produced   The end result and the desired value in the eyes of the customer

Processes account for 90% of why our results are what they are. The who, the special excuses… those are all just in the 10%. So, if want to improve, we need to improve the PROCESS.

We're not talking procedures here. We're talking about the *way* stuff gets done. Processes are what really happens. They may or MAY NOT be the same as the procedures.

In pursuing excellence, we focus on improving our underlying processes, most of which are ingrained in our habits. To help us in that effort, we make the process visible with a map.

Process maps are the core tool for every process improvement methodology, including Six Sigma and LEAN. Talking about process issues or improvements without a process map would be like remodeling your house without any sketches.

    Step 1: Draw the SIPOC – *Suppliers-Inputs-Process (transformation)-Output-Outcomes (customers)* **– version first.** This is the process map that shows the fundamental purpose of the process.

Focus first on how inputs are transformed into outputs. That is the core activity or mission of the process.

Next, explicitly state the desired outcomes. These are the intangible reasons that customers pay for a process to exist.

The C, meanwhile, stands for both outCome and Customer. The outcome is the deep purpose that creates the connection for the buyer. An <u>outcome</u> differs from an <u>output</u> in that it's usually intangible. A common way to keep these distinct is that you can drop an output on your toe or make a movie of it.

Step 2: **Map out the flow of activities**. As the process improvement effort requires, be ready to identify the value of each step, its cycle time, its effort and its outputs.

Step 3: **Validate the map** with the actual owners and doers of each process step.

Speed Team Building

Why Use: To get to know your teammates beyond their resumés.

When to Use: During concept development and when exploring ideas for changes or revisions to the current plan.

Welcome to the team-building exercise that, when introduced, makes most people want to be invisible… yet, when it's over, results in most people having eye-opening, trust-building connections with other team members.

Pre-event setup: Set up chairs in two lines facing each other, with each pair separated by enough space for it to feel like a crowded restaurant, not a city bus. Randomly assign who sits in which chair without any appearance of pretense. Otherwise, it really messes with the dynamics. Don't do it.

If you have an odd number of people, have one person be an observer who watches everyone's body language and reports back to everyone at the end of the round. This person can then rotate into the conversations for the next round.

A sample instructions script: We'll be doing some high-speed, high-intensity team building. You'll be having one-on-one conversation events with a person across from you. And we'll have several of these events so you can have several conversation partners during this entire exercise.

I'll give you a kick-starter topic to talk about, and then you'll have five minutes for both of you to share your thoughts on it. Please be respectful of each other and don't suck up all the airtime.

Here are the guidelines for the conversation…

What each person WILL talk about:

- Personal perspectives on the topic
- Personal aspirations
- Reflective answers to deep questions.

What each person WILL NOT talk about:

- Anything from today's news
- Anything found on your resumé
- Your day-to-day job / Issues going on at work
- Where you live or lived
- Facts that are Google-able about you.

At the end of each conversation event, I'll ask a few conversation pairs to share what they discussed. Then we'll rotate conversation partners and have another conversation – maybe with a new topic, maybe the same.

Facilitator guidelines between conversation events: Once the time is up for that round (i.e., five minutes), bring the group's attention back to you.

Ask one or two duos (four people max) to share their partner's response to the prompt. A good rule of thumb is to first ask a pair that seemed serious and focused, and then a pair that were having a great time while they talked. Also, if you have one, ask the observer to share his/her observations.

Objectives in asking these questions: 1) Expands the storytelling to broaden the group experience. 2) Gives accountability for listening, rather than just waiting to speak. 3) Allows everyone to experience something together.

Rotating Conversation Partners: Since participants have likely over-heard some of the talk around them, have one side of the partners move down at least 2-3 chairs for the next round. This maximizes their exposure to others on the team. Make sure to rotate the observer as well (if you have one).

Post-Event Debrief: Ask if participants were surprised by what they learned about your teammates? What new information did they gather about the larger team?

Draw on the teams' answers to illustrate your objectives to conduct the exercise in the first place. This is your opportunity to discuss the value of a high-trust team, and here's a cheat sheet for some things you might have seen and can therefore address.

- Participants seeing a new side of their teammates
- Laughing together (an indicator of new brain connections)
- Vulnerability to share with one another
- New people being brought into the culture of the team
- Experienced people seeing value in new perspectives.

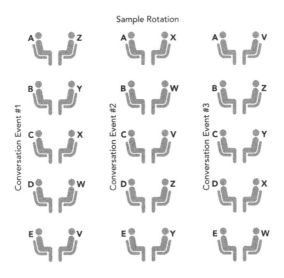

Sample Rotation

Why do we have rules for what we can talk about?

This event is designed to help teams get a better sense of the people on the team – their disposition, character and "way of being in the world." Often, we only get to hear facts and figures about people: where they grew up, how many siblings they have, what they majored in, where they work, etc.

These stats are something, yes. But they don't effectively build team trust. For that, we have to get a layer deeper. That's what speed team building does.

Why have one-on-one conversations?

People may recognize this format as "speed dating" style, and that is true. We set it up this way because one-on-one conversations are the most valuable in building relationships in a team. As those relationships develop and the stories are told, the team becomes more closely knit

Think Aloud Testing

Why Use: To solicit customer responses and reactions in order to discern how to better satisfy customer needs and delight the customer.

When to Use: During concept development and when exploring ideas for changes or revisions to the current plan.

To employ this method, put the idea on a poster-sized paper or projected on a wall. Use as many pictures as possible.

Invite the customer to come and take a look at it. Give them a seat, a drink and a snack to make them comfortable when they do.

Request the customer to think out loud, verbally expressing each and every thought going through his/her mind, even if the thought is, "What in the world is that?!?!?" or "What am I looking at?"

Meanwhile, you and/or a couple members of your team stay BEHIND the customer, listening intently and jotting down EVERYTHING you hear. Don't question. Don't defend. Just listen and write.

Give the customer ample time. Even encourage them to stay a bit longer, asking if there's anything else he/she would like to share. All the while, neither defend nor promote the idea(s) being commented on. This is only an exercise to hear the customer reactions, not a formal design review.

Ask the customer if he/she would like to do this again at the next stage, or whether he/she sees a benefit to a more formal review later.

You and your team can also share what you heard. Again, there's no defenses allowed. The main purpose is to assure the customer of what you and your team heard so that there's less risk of misrecording or misinterpreting. You do not ask the customer why they said any of what they said, only looking for confirmation.

At the end, thank the customer.

During this observation/interaction, note how you saw the customer's body language and mood evolve from first reaction to understanding to appreciating (or disliking).

Note that you can complement this tool with the Kano Mapping tool.

Helping Christ carry His Cross
fills one with a strong and pure joy,
and those who may and can do so,
the builders of God's Kingdom,
are the most authentic children of God.

—Edith Stein, aka Sr. Teresa Benedicta of the Cross, O.C.D.
German Jewish philosopher, one-time atheist
Martyred in Auschwitz, 1942

References

1   Achor, Shawn. The Happiness Advantage, Crown, 2010.
2   Baumeister, Roy. The meanings of life:Happiness is not the same as a sense of meaning. How do we go about finding a meaningful life, not just a happy one? Aeon essays, 2013.
3   Briggs, Isabel. Gifts Differing: Understanding Personality Type. Myers-Davies-Black Publishing. 1995.
4   Cooper, Robert G. Winning at New Products, Basic Books, 2017.
5   Deming, W. Edwards. Out of the Crisis, MIT Press, 1982.
6   Deming, W. Edwards. The New Economics for Industry, Government, Education, 2nd Ed., MIT Press, 1994.
7   Frankl, Viktor, Man's Search for Meaning. Beacon Press, 2006.
8   Greenleaf, Robert. The Servant as Leader, pamphlet, The Greenleaf Center for Servant Leadership, 2015.
9   Heath, Chip and Heath, Dan. Switch: How to Change Things When Change is Hard, Crown Business, 2010.
10 Herzberg, Frederick, "One More Time: How Do You Motivate Employees?" (Reprint R0301F), Harvard Business Review, 1968.
11 Joiner, Brian and Streibel, Barbara. The Team Handbook, Joiner, 1996.
12 Kahnemann, Daniel. Thinking Fast and Slow, Farrar, Straus and Giroux, 2011.
13 Kelly, Matthew. The Dream Manager. Hyperion, 2007.
14 Kidder, Tracy. The Soul of a New Machine, Little Brown and Company, 1981.
15 Kotter, John. Leading Change, Harvard Business School Press, 1996.
16 Lencioni, Patrick. Five Dysfunctions of a Team, Jossey-Bass, 2002.
17 Lencioni, Patrick. Three Signs of a Miserable Job, Wiley.
18 Lewis, C.S. The Space Trilotgy, Simon & Schuster; Reissue edition, 2011.
19 Lewis, C.S. Surprised by Joy, HarperOne; Reissue edition, 2017.
20 Maxwell, John C. The 21 Irrefutable Laws of Leadership: Follow Them and People Will Follow You, Nelson, 2007.
21 Neave, Henry R. The Deming Dimension, SPC Press, 1990.
22 Pirsig, Robert M. Zen and the Art of Motorcycle Maintenance, 1974.
23 Patterson, Kerry; Grenny, Joseph; McMillan, Ron; Switzler, Al, Crucial Conversations, McGraw-Hill Education, 2011.
24 PMBOK® Guide – Sixth Edition, 2017
25 PMI *2013 Pulse of the Profession^{TM} Report.*
26 Pope Francis. The Joy of the Gospel, Image, 2014.
27 Senge, Peter. The Fifth Discipline: The Art & Practice of The Learning Organization 2006.
28 Senge, Peter et. al. Fifth Discipline Fieldbook, Crown Business, 1994.
29 Sinek, Simon. Start with Why: How Great Leaders Inspire Everyone to Take Action, Portfolio Trade, 2011.
30 Walton, Mary.The Deming Management Method, Perigee Books, 1988.
31 Walton, Mary. Deming Management at Work, Perigee Books, 1991

Edith Stein quote was taken from The Collected Works of Edith Stein, Vol. IV, Edited by Dr. L. Gelber and Michael Linssenm O.C.D, ICS Publications, 1992.

ABOUT THE AUTHOR

Paul Armstrong has pursued understanding the power of enabling joy for nearly three decades. With a background in engineering, he has worked with leaders and project teams across a range of businesses, primarily in rigorous technologies where failure is not an option. His first book, *Enabling Joy*, is a fictional story based on real experiences that reveals how good leaders with various personalities come to grips with enabling joy, both on the job and in their personal lives.

Paul is founder and partner of eNthusaProve, LLC, a consultancy that helps team leaders find ways to enable joy and engage excellence. He resides in Lancaster, PA with his bride of over 30 years, where they nurture a small farm and giggle with grandchildren.

Made in the USA
Middletown, DE
07 January 2020